LINUX

The Ultimate Step by Step Guide to Quickly and Easily Learning Linux

TED DAWSON

Chapter One: LINUX HISTORY

The history of Linux began in 1991 with the commencement of a personal project by Finnish student Linus Torvalds to create a new free operating system kernel. Since then, the resulting Linux kernel has been marked by constant growth throughout its history. Since the initial release of its source code in 1991, it has grown from a small number of C files under a license prohibiting commercial distribution to the 3.18 version in 2015 with more than 18 million lines of source code under the GNU General Public License (GPL). He wrote the program specifically for the hardware he was using and independent of an operating system because he wanted to use the functions of his new PC with an Intel 80386 processor. Development was done on MINIX using the GNU C compiler. The GNU C Compiler is still the main choice for compiling Linux today. The code can be built with other compilers, such as the Intel C Compiler. As Torvalds wrote in his book 'Just for Fun,' he eventually ended up writing an operating system kernel. On 25 August 1991 (age 21), he announced this new system in a Usenet posting to the newsgroup "comp.os.minix."

Torvalds first published the Linux kernel under its own license, which had a restriction on commercial activity. The software used with the kernel was developed as part of the GNU project licensed under the GNU GPL, a free software license. The first release of the Linux kernel, Linux 0.01, included a binary of GNU's Bash shell. In the "Notes for Linux release 0.01", Torvalds lists the GNU software that is required to run Linux: Sadly, a kernel by itself gets you nowhere. To get a working system, you need a shell, compilers, a library, etc. These are separate parts and may be under stricter (or even looser) copyright. Most of the tools used with Linux are GNU software and are under the GNU copyright. These tools are not in the distribution - ask me (or GNU) for more info. In 1992, he suggested releasing the kernel under the GNU GPL. He first announced this decision in the release notes of version 0.12. In the middle of December 1992, he published version 0.99 using the GNU GPL. Linux and GNU developers worked to integrate GNU components with Linux to make a fully functional free operating system. Torvalds has stated, "Making Linux GPL'd was definitely the best thing I ever did." Torvalds initially used the designation "Linux" only for the Linux kernel. The kernel was, however, frequently used together with other software, especially that of the GNU project. This quickly became the most popular adoption of GNU software. In June 1994 in GNU's Bulletin, Linux was referred to as a "free UNIX clone," and the Debian project began calling its product Debian GNU/Linux. In May 1996, Richard Stallman published the editor Emacs 19.31, in which the type of system was renamed from Linux to Lignux. This spelling was intended to refer specifically to the combination of GNU and Linux, but this was soon abandoned in favor of "GNU/Linux." This name garnered varying reactions. The GNU and Debian projects use the name, although most people simply use the term "Linux" to refer to the combination.

The largest part of the work on Linux is performed by the community: the thousands of programmers around the world that use Linux to send their suggested improvements to the maintainers. Various companies have also helped not only with the development of the kernels but also with the writing the body of auxiliary software, which is distributed with Linux. As of February 2015, over 80% of Linux kernel developers are paid. It is released both by organized projects such as Debian and by projects connected directly with companies such as Fedora and openSUSE. The members of these respective projects meet at various conferences and fairs, in order to exchange ideas. One of the largest of these fairs is the LinuxTag in Germany (currently in Berlin), where about 10,000 people assemble annually, in order to discuss Linux and the projects associated with it. The Open Source Development Lab (OSDL) was created in the year 2000, and is an independent nonprofit organization, which pursues the goal of optimizing Linux for employment in data centers and in the carrier range. It served as sponsored working premises for Linus Torvalds and also for Andrew Morton (until the middle of 2006 when Morton transferred to Google). Torvalds worked full-time on behalf of OSDL, developing the Linux kernels.

Chronology

1991: The Linux kernel is publicly announced on 25 August by 21-year-old Finnish student Linus Benedict Torvalds.

1992: The Linux kernel is re-licensed under the GNU GPL. The first Linux distributions are created.

1993: Over 100 developers work on the Linux kernel. With their assistance, the kernel is adapted to the GNU environment, which creates a large spectrum of application types for Linux. The oldest currently (as of 2015) existing Linux distribution, Slackware, is released for the first time. Later that same year, the Debian project is established. Today it is the largest distribution community.

1994: Torvalds judges all components of the kernel to be fully matured: he releases version 1.0 of Linux. The XFree86 project contributes a graphical user interface (GUI). Commercial Linux distribution makers Red Hat and SUSE publish version 1.0 of their Linux distributions.

1995: Linux is ported to the DEC Alpha and the Sun SPARC systems. Over the following years, it is ported to an ever-greater number of platforms.

1996: Version 2.0 of the Linux kernel is released. The kernel can now serve several processors at the same time using symmetric multi-processing (SMP), and thereby becomes a serious alternative for many companies.

1998: Many major companies such as IBM, Compaq, and Oracle announce their support for Linux. The Cathedral and the Bazaar were first published as an essay (later as a book), resulting in Netscape publicly releasing the source code to its Netscape Communicator web browser suite. Netscape's actions and crediting of the essay brings Linux's open source development model to the attention of the popular technical press. In addition, a group of programmers began developing the graphical user interface KDE.

1999: A group of developers began work on the graphical environment GNOME, destined to become a free replacement for KDE, which at the time depended on the then proprietary, Qt GUI toolkit. During this year, IBM announced an extensive project for the support of Linux.

2000: Dell announces that it is now the No. 2 provider of Linux-based systems worldwide and the first major manufacturer to offer Linux across its full product line.

2002: The media reported, "Microsoft killed Dell Linux."

2004: The XFree86 team splits up and joins with the existing X standards body to form the X.Org Foundation, which results in a substantially faster development of the X server for Linux.

2005: The project openSUSE begins free distribution from Novell's community. In addition, the project OpenOffice.org introduces version 2.0 which then started supporting OASIS OpenDocument standards.

2006: Oracle releases its own distribution of Red Hat Enterprise Linux. Novell and Microsoft announce cooperation for better interoperability and mutual patent protection.

2007: Dell starts distributing laptops with Ubuntu pre-installed.

2009: Red Hats market capitalization equals Suns, interpreted as a symbolic moment for the "Linux-based economy."

2011: Version 3.0 of the Linux kernel is released.

2012: The aggregate Linux server market revenue exceeds that of the rest of the UNIX market.

2013: Google's Linux-based Android claims 75% of the Smartphone market share, in terms of the number of phones shipped.

2014: Ubuntu claims 22,000,000 users.

2015: Version 4.0 of the Linux kernel is released.

Chapter Two: LINUX DISTRIBUTION (DISTRO)

Introduction

The bewildering choice and the ever increasing number of Linux distributions can be confusing for those who are new to Linux. This is why this book was created. It lists 10 Linux distributions (plus an honorable mention of FreeBSD, by far the most popular of all of the BSDs), it is considered to be the most widely-used by Linux users around the world. There are no figures to back up this claim, and there are many other distributions that might suit your particular purpose better, but as a general rule, all of these are popular and have very active forums or mailing lists where you can ask questions if you get stuck. Ubuntu, Linux Mint, and PCLinuxOS are considered the easiest for new users who want to get productive in Linux as soon as possible without having to master all of its complexities. On the other end of the spectrum, Slackware Linux, Arch Linux, and FreeBSD are more advanced distributions that require a deeper understanding, before they can be used effectively. openSUSE, Fedora, Debian GNU/Linux and Mageia can be classified as good "middle-road" distributions. CentOS is an enterprise distribution, suitable for those who prefer stability, reliability, and long-term support to cutting-edge features and software.

GUIDE TO CHOOSING DISTRIBUTION

Linux Mint

Linux Mint, a distribution based on Ubuntu, was first launched in 2006 by Clement Lefebvre, a French-born IT specialist living in Ireland. Originally maintaining a Linux web site dedicated to providing help, tips and documentation to new Linux users, the author saw the potential of developing a Linux distribution that would address the many usability drawbacks associated with the generally more technical, mainstream products. Since its beginnings, the developers have been adding a variety of graphical "mint" tools for enhanced usability; this includes mintDesktop - a utility for configuring the desktop environment, mintMenu - a new and elegant menu structure for easier navigation, mintInstall - an easy-to-use software installer, and mintUpdate - a software updater. Mint's reputation for ease of use has been further enhanced by the inclusion of proprietary and patent-encumbered multimedia codecs that are often absent from larger distributions due to potential legal threats. Perhaps one of the best features of Linux Mint is the fact that the developers listen to the users and are always fast in implementing good suggestions. While Linux Mint is available as a free download, the project generates revenue from donations, advertising, and professional support services.

Pros: Superb collection of "minty" tools developed in-house, hundreds of user-friendly enhancements, the inclusion of multimedia codecs, open to users' suggestions.

Cons: The alternative "community" editions do not always include the latest features; the project does not issue security advisories.

Ubuntu

The launch of Ubuntu was first announced in September 2004. Although a relative newcomer to the Linux distribution scene, the project took off like no other, with its mailing lists soon filled with discussions by eager users and enthusiastic developers. In the years that followed, Ubuntu grew to become the most popular desktop Linux distribution and has contributed greatly toward developing an easy-to-use and free desktop operating system that can compete well with any of the proprietary ones available on the market. On the technical side of things, Ubuntu is based on Debian "Sid" (unstable branch), but with some prominent packages, such as GNOME, Firefox, and LibreOffice, updated to their latest versions. It uses a custom user interface called "Unity." It has a predictable, 6-month release schedule, with an occasional Long Term Support (LTS) release that is supports security updates for 5 years, depending on the edition (non-LTS release are supported for 9 months). Other special features of Ubuntu include an installable live DVD, creative artwork, desktop themes, migration assistant for Windows users, support for the latest technologies, such as 3D desktop effects, easy installation of proprietary device drivers for ATI and NVIDIA graphics cards, wireless networking, and on-demand support for non-free or patent-encumbered media codecs.

Pros: Fixed release cycle and support period; long-term support (LTS) variants with 5 years of security updates; novice-friendly; a wealth of documentation, both official and user-contributed.

Cons: Lacks compatibility with Debian; frequent major changes tend to drive some users away, the Unity user interface has been criticized as being more suitable for mobile devices rather than desktop computers; non-LTS releases come with only 9 months of security support.

Debian GNU/Linux

Debian GNU/Linux was first announced in 1993. Its founder, Ian Murdock, envisaged the creation of a completely non-commercial product developed by hundreds of volunteer developers. With skeptics far outnumbering optimists at the time, it seemed destined to disintegrate and collapse, but the reality was very different. Debian not only survived, it thrived and, in less than a decade, it became the largest Linux distribution and possibly the largest collaborative software product ever created! The following numbers can illustrate the success of Debian GNU/Linux. Over 1,000 volunteer developers develop it, its software repositories contain close to 50,000 binary packages (compiled for 8 processor architectures) and is responsible for inspiring over 120 Debian-based distributions and live CDs. These figures are unmatched by any other Linux-based operating system. The actual development of Debian takes place in three main branches (or four if one includes the bleeding-edge "experimental" branch) of increasing levels of stability: "unstable" (also known as "sid"), "testing" and "stable." However, this lengthy and complex development style has some drawbacks: the stable releases of Debian are not particularly up-to-date, and they age rapidly, especially since new stable releases are only published once every 1 - 3 years. Users who prefer the latest packages and technologies are forced to use the potentially buggy Debian testing distributions or unstable branches. The highly democratic structures of Debian have led to controversial decisions and have led to infighting among the developers. This has contributed to stagnation and reluctance to make radical decisions that would take the project forward.

Pros: Very stable; remarkable quality control; includes over 30,000 software packages; supports more processor architectures than any other Linux distribution.

Cons: Conservative - due to its support for many processor architectures, newer technologies are not always included; slow release cycle (one stable release every 1 - 3 years); discussions on developer mailing lists and blogs can be uncultured at times.

Mageia

Mageia may be the newest distribution on this list, but its roots go back to July 1998 when Gaël Duval launched Mandrake Linux. At the time, it was just a branch of Red Hat Linux with KDE as the default desktop, better hardware detection, and some user-friendly features, but it gained instant popularity due to positive reviews in the media. Mandrake was later turned into a commercial enterprise and renamed to Mandriva (to avoid some trademark-related hassles and to celebrate its merger with Brazil's Conectiva) before almost going bankrupt in 2010. A Russian venture capital firm eventually saved it, but this came at a cost when the new management decided to lay off most of the established Mandriva developers in the company's Paris headquarters. Upon finding themselves out of work, they decided to form Mageia, a community project that is a logical continuation of Mandrake and Mandriva, perhaps more so than Mandriva itself. Mageia is primarily a desktop distribution. Its best-loved features are cutting-edge software, a superb system administration suite (Mageia Control Centre), the ability to attract a large number of volunteer contributors, and extensive internationalization support. It features one of the easiest, but more powerful system installers on its installation DVD, while it also releases a set of live images with both KDE or GNOME desktops and comprehensive language support, with the ability to install it onto a hard disk directly from the live desktop session. The distribution's well-established package management features, with powerful command-line options and a graphical software management module, allow easy access to thousands of software packages. The unique Mageia Control Center continues to improve with each release, offering a powerful tool for configuring just about any aspect of their computer without ever reaching for the terminal.

Pros: Beginner-friendly; excellent central configuration utility; very good out-of-the-box support for dozens of languages; installable live media.

Cons: Lacks reputation and mindshare following its split from Mandriva, some concern over the developers' ability to maintain the distribution long-term on a volunteer basis.

Fedora

Although Fedora was formally only unveiled in September 2004, its origins date back to 1995 when it was launched by two Linux visionaries -- Bob Young and Marc Ewing -- under the name of Red Hat Linux. The company's first product, Red Hat Linux 1.0 "Mother's Day," was released the same year and was quickly followed by several bug-fix updates. In 1997, Red Hat introduced its revolutionary RPM package management system with dependency resolution and other advanced features which greatly contributed to the distribution's rapid rise in popularity and its overtaking of Slackware Linux as the most widely-used Linux distribution in the world. In later years, Red Hat standardized on a regular, 6-month release schedule. In 2003, just after the release of Red Hat Linux 9, the company introduced some radical changes to its product line-up. It retained the Red Hat trademark for its commercial products, notably Red Hat Enterprise Linux, and introduced Fedora Core (later renamed to Fedora), a Red Hat sponsored, but community-oriented distribution designed for the "Linux hobbyist". After the initial criticism of the changes, the Linux community accepted the "new" distribution as the logical continuation of Red Hat Linux. A few quality releases was all it took for Fedora to regain its former status as one of the best-loved operating systems on the market. At the same time, Red Hat quickly became the biggest and most profitable Linux company in the world, with an innovative product line-up, excellent customer support, and other popular initiatives, such as its Red Hat Certified Engineer (RHCE) certification program. Although Fedora's direction is still largely controlled by Red Hat, Inc. and the product is sometimes seen -- rightly or wrongly -- as a test bed for Red Hat Enterprise Linux, there is no denying that Fedora is one of the most innovative distributions available today. Its contributions to the Linux kernel, glibc and GCC are well-known and its more recent integration of SELinux functionality, virtualization technologies, system service manager, cutting-edge journaled file systems, and other enterprise-level features are much appreciated by the company's customers. On a negative side, Fedora still lacks a clear desktop-oriented strategy that would make the product easier to use for those beyond the "Linux hobbyist" target.

Pros: Highly innovative; outstanding security features; a large number of supported packages; strict adherence to the free software philosophy; availability of live CDs featuring many popular desktop environments.

Cons: Fedora's priorities tend to lean towards enterprise features, rather than desktop usability; some bleeding edge features, such as early switch to KDE 4 and GNOME 3, occasionally alienate desktop users.

openSUSE

The beginnings of openSUSE date back to 1992 when four German Linux enthusiasts -- Roland Dyroff, Thomas Fehr, Hubert Mantel and Burchard Steinbild -- launched the project under the name of SUSE (Software und System Entwicklung) Linux. In the early days, the young company sold sets of floppy disks containing a German edition of Slackware Linux, but it wasn't long before SUSE Linux became an independent distribution with the launch of version 4.2 in May 1996. In the following years, the developers adopted the RPM package management format and introduced YaST, an easy-to-use graphical system administration tool. Frequent releases, excellent printed documentation, and easy availability of SUSE Linux in stores across Europe and North America resulted in growing popularity of the distribution. SUSE Linux was acquired by Novell, Inc. in late 2003, and then fell into the hands of Attachmate in November 2010. Major changes in the development, licensing and availability of SUSE Linux followed shortly after the first acquisition - YaST was released under the GPL, the ISO images were freely distributed from public download servers, and, most significantly, the development of the distribution was opened to public participation for the first time. Since the launch of the openSUSE project and the release of version 10.0 in October 2005, the distribution became completely free in both senses of the word. The openSUSE code has become a base system for

Novell's commercial products, first named as Novell Linux, but later renamed to SUSE Linux Enterprise Desktop and SUSE Linux Enterprise Server. Today, openSUSE has a large following of satisfied users. The principal reason for openSUSE receiving high marks from its users are pleasant and polished desktop environments (KDE and GNOME), an excellent system administration utility (YaST), and, for those who buy the boxed edition, some of the best-printed documentation available. However, the infamous deal between Novell and Microsoft, which apparently concedes to Microsoft's argument that it has intellectual property rights over Linux, has resulted in condemnation by many Linux personalities and has prompted some users to switch distributions. Although Novell has downplayed the deal, and Microsoft has yet to exercise any rights, this issue remains a thorn in the side of the otherwise very community-friendly Linux Company.

Pros: Comprehensive and intuitive configuration tool; large repository of software packages, excellent web site infrastructure, and printed documentation.

Cons: Novell's patent deal with Microsoft in November 2006 seemingly legitimized Microsoft's intellectual property claims over Linux; its resource-heavy desktop set-up and graphical utilities are sometimes seen as "bloated and slow."

Arch Linux

The KISS (Keep It Simple, Stupid) philosophy of Arch Linux was devised around the year 2002 by Judd Vinet, a Canadian computer science graduate who launched the distribution the same year. For several years it lived as a marginal project designed for intermediate and advanced Linux users and only shot to stardom when it began promoting itself as a "rolling-release" distribution that only needs to be installed once and is then kept up-to-date thanks to its powerful package manager and an always fresh software repository. As a result, Arch Linux "releases" are few and far between and are now limited to a basic installation DVD that is issued only when considerable changes in the base system warrant a fresh install. Besides featuring the much-loved "rolling-release" update mechanism, Arch Linux is also renowned for its fast and powerful package manager called "Pacman", the ability to install software packages from source code, easy creation of binary packages thanks to its AUR infrastructure, and the ever increasing software repository of well-tested packages. Its highly regarded documentation, complemented by the excellent Arch Linux Handbook makes it possible for even less experienced Linux users to install and customize the distribution. The powerful tools available at the user's disposal mean that the distro is infinitely customizable to the minutest detail and that no two installations can possibly be the same. On the negative side, any rolling-release update mechanism has its dangers: a human mistake can creep in, a library or dependency goes missing, a new version of an application already in the repository has a yet-to-be-reported critical bug... It is not unheard of to end up with an unbootable system following a Pacman upgrade. As such, Arch Linux is the kind of distribution that requires its users to be alert and to have enough knowledge to fix any such problems. In addition, the infrequent install media releases mean that it is sometimes no longer possible to use the old media to install the distribution due to important system changes or lack of hardware support in the older Linux kernel.

Pros: Excellent software management infrastructure; unparalleled customization and tweaking options; superb online documentation.

Cons: Occasional instability and risk of breakdown.

CentOS

Launched in late 2003, CentOS is a community project with the goals of rebuilding the source code for Red Hat Enterprise Linux (RHEL) into an installable Linux distribution and to provide timely security updates for all included software packages. To put in more bluntly, CentOS is an RHEL clone. The only technical difference between the two distributions is branding - CentOS replaced all Red Hat trademarks and logos with its own. Nevertheless, the relations between Red Hat and CentOS remain amicable, and many CentOS developers are in active contact with, or even employed directly by, Red Hat. CentOS is often seen as a reliable server distribution. It comes with the same well-tested and stable Linux kernel and set of software packages that form the basis of its parent, Red Hat Enterprise Linux. Despite being a community project run by volunteers, it has gained a reputation for being a solid, free alternative to more costly server products on the market, especially among experienced Linux system administrators. CentOS is also suitable as an enterprise desktop solution, specifically where stability, reliability and long-term support are preferred over latest software and new features, like RHEL, CentOS includes approximately 7-10 years of security updates. Despite its advantages, CentOS might not be the best solution in all deployment scenarios. Those users who prefer a distribution with the latest Linux technologies and newest software packages should look elsewhere. Major CentOS versions, which follow RHEL versioning, are only released every 2 - 3 years, while "point" releases (e.g. 5.1) tend to arrive in 6 - 9 month intervals. The point releases do not usually contain any major features (although they do sometimes include support for more recent hardware), and only a handful of software packages may get updated to newer versions. The Linux kernel, the base system, and most application versions remain unchanged, but occasionally a newer version of an important software package (e.g. LibreOffice or Firefox) may be provided on an experimental basis. As a side project, CentOS also builds updated packages for the users of its distributions, but the repositories containing them are not enabled by default as they may break upstream compatibility.

Pros: Extremely well tested, stable and reliable; free to download and use; comes with 7+ years of free security updates.

Cons: Lacks latest Linux technologies; occasionally the project fails to live up its.

PCLinuxOS

Bill "Texstar" Reynolds first introduced PCLinuxOS in 2003. Prior to creating his own distribution, Texstar was already a well-known developer in the Mandrake Linux community of users for building up-to-date RPM packages for the popular distribution and providing them as a free download. In 2003, he decided to build a new distribution, initially based on Mandrake Linux, but with several significant usability improvements. The goals? It should be beginner-friendly, have out-of-the box support for proprietary kernel modules, browser plug-in and media codecs, and should function as a live CD with a simple and intuitive graphical installer. Several years and development releases later, PCLinuxOS is rapidly approaching its intended state. In terms of usability, the project offers out-of-the-box support for many technologies that most Windows-to-Linux migrants would expect from a new operating system. On the software side of things, PCLinuxOS is a KDE-oriented distribution, with a customized and always up-to-date version of the popular desktop environment. Its growing software repository contains other desktops and offers a great variety of desktop packages for many common tasks. For system configuration, PCLinuxOS has retained much of Mandriva's excellent Control Centre but has replaced its package management system with APT and Synaptic, a graphical package management front-end. On the negative side, PCLinuxOS lacks any form of roadmap or release goals. Despite growing community involvement, most development and decision-making remains in the hands of Texstar, who tends to be conservative when judging the stability of a release. As a result, the development process of PCLinuxOS is often arduous. For example, despite frequent calls for a 64-bit edition, the developers held off producing a 64-bit build until fairly recently. Furthermore, the project does not provide any security advisories, relying instead on the users' willingness to keep their system up-to-date via the included package management tools.

Pros: Out-of-the-box support for graphics drivers, browser plug-ins, and media codecs; rolling-release update mechanism; up-to-date software.

Cons: no out-of-the-box support for non-English languages; lacks release planning and security advisories.

Slackware Linux

Slackware Linux, created by Patrick Volkerding in 1992, is the oldest surviving Linux distribution. Separated from the now-discontinued SLS project, Slackware 1.0 came on 24 floppy disks and was built on top of Linux kernel version 0.99pl11-alpha. It quickly became the most popular Linux distribution; with some estimates putting its market share as much as 80% of all Linux installations in 1995. Its popularity decreased dramatically with the arrival of Red Hat Linux and other, user-friendlier distributions, but Slackware Linux still remains a much-appreciated operating system among the more technically oriented system administrators and desktop users. Slackware Linux is a highly technical, clean distribution, with only a limited number of custom utilities. It uses a simple, text-based system installer and a comparatively primitive package management system that does not resolve software dependencies. As a result, Slackware is considered one of the cleanest and least buggy distributions available today - the lack of Slackware-specific enhancements reduces the likelihood of new bugs being introduced into the system. The entire system configuration is completed by editing text files. There is a saying in the Linux community that if you learn Red Hat, you'll know Red Hat, but if you learn

Slackware, you'll know Linux. This is particularly true today when many other Linux distributions keep developing heavily customized products to meet the needs of less technical Linux users. While this philosophy of simplicity has its fans, the fact is that in today's world, Slackware Linux is increasingly becoming a "core system" upon which new, custom solutions are built, rather than a complete distribution with a wide variety of supported software. The only exception is the server market, where Slackware remains popular, though even here, the distribution's complex upgrade procedure and lack of officially supported automated tools for security updates make it increasingly uncompetitive. Slackware's conservative attitude towards the system's base components means that it requires much manual post-installation work before it can be turned into a modern desktop system.

Pros: Considered highly stable, clean and largely bug-free, strong adherence to UNIX principles.

Cons: Limited number of officially supported applications; conservative in terms of base package selection; complex upgrade procedure.

FreeBSD

FreeBSD, an indirect descendant of AT&T UNIX via the Berkeley Software Distribution (BSD), has a long and turbulent history dating back to 1993. Unlike Linux distributions, which are defined as integrated software solutions consisting of the Linux kernel and thousands of software applications, FreeBSD is a tightly integrated operating system built from a BSD kernel and the so-called "userland" (therefore usable even without extra applications). This distinction is largely lost once installed on the average computer system - like many Linux distributions, a large collection of easily installed, (mostly) open source applications are available for extending the FreeBSD core, but these are usually provided by third-party contributors and aren't strictly part of FreeBSD. FreeBSD has developed a reputation for being a fast, high-performance and extremely stable operating system, especially suitable for web serving and similar tasks. Many large web search engines and organizations with mission-critical computing infrastructures have deployed and used FreeBSD on their computer systems for years. Compared to Linux, FreeBSD is distributed under a much less restrictive license, which allows virtually unrestricted use and modification of the source code for any purpose. Even Apple's Mac OS X is known to have been derived from FreeBSD. Besides the core operating system, the project also provides over 24,000 software applications in binary and source code forms for easy installation on top of the core FreeBSD. While FreeBSD can certainly be used as a desktop operating system, although it does not compare well to more popular Linux distributions. The text-mode system installer offers little in terms of hardware detection or system configuration, leaving much of the dirty work to the user in a post-installation setup. In terms of support for modern hardware, FreeBSD generally lags behind Linux, especially in supporting cutting-edge desktop and laptop gadgets, such as wireless network cards or digital cameras. Those users seeking to exploit the speed and stability of FreeBSD on a desktop or workstation should consider one of the available desktop FreeBSD projects, rather than FreeBSD itself.

Pros: Fast and stable; availability of over 24,000 software applications (or "ports") for installation; very good documentation.

Cons: Tends to lag behind Linux in terms of support for new and exotic hardware, limited availability of commercial applications; lacks graphical configuration tools.

Chapter Three: LICENSING

Code is contributed to the Linux kernel under a number of licenses, but all code must be compatible with version 2 of the GNU (GPLv2), which is the license covering the kernel distribution as a whole. In practice, that means that all code contributions are covered either by GPLv2 (with, optionally, language allowing distribution under later versions of the GPL) or the three-clause BSD license. Any contributions, which are not covered by a compatible license, will not be accepted into the kernel. Copyright assignments are not required (or requested) for code contributed to the kernel. All code merged into the mainline kernel retains its original ownership; as a result, the kernel now has thousands of owners. One implication of this ownership structure is that any attempt to change the licensing of the kernel is doomed to almost certain failure. There are few practical scenarios where the agreement of all copyright holders could be obtained (or their code removed from the kernel). Therefore, there is no prospect of a migration to version 3 of the GPL in the foreseeable future. It is imperative that all code contributed to the kernel be legitimately free software. For that reason, code from anonymous (or pseudonymous) contributors will not be accepted.

All contributors are required to "sign off" on their code, stating that the code can be distributed with the kernel under the GPL. Code which its owner, has not licensed as free software, or which risks creating copyright-related problems for the kernel (such as code which derives from reverse-engineering efforts lacking proper safeguards) cannot be contributed. Questions about copyright-related issues are common on Linux development mailing lists. Such questions will normally receive no shortage of answers, but one should bear in mind that the people answering those questions are not lawyers and cannot provide legal advice. If you have legal questions relating to Linux source code, there is no substitute for talking with a lawyer who understands this field. Relying on answers obtained on technical mailing lists is a risky affair.

COMMUNITY

Linux communities come in two basic forms: developer and user.

One of the most compelling features of Linux is that it is accessible to developers; anybody with the requisite skills can improve Linux and influence the direction of its development. Proprietary products cannot offer this kind of openness, which is a characteristic of the free software process. Developer communities can volunteer to maintain and support whole distributions, such as the Debian or Gentoo Projects. Novell and Red Hat also support community-driven versions of their products, openSUSE and Fedora, respectively. The improvements to these community distros are then incorporated into the commercial server and desktop products. The Linux kernel itself is primarily supported by its developer community and is one of the largest and most active free software projects in existence. A typical three-month kernel development cycle can involve over 1000 developers working for more than 100 different companies (or for no company at all).

With the growth of Linux has come an increase in the number of developers (and companies) wishing to participate in its development. Hardware vendors want to ensure that Linux supports their products well, making their products attractive to Linux users. Embedded systems vendors, who use Linux as a component in an integrated product, want Linux to be as capable and well suited to the task at hand as possible. Distributors and other software vendors who base their products on Linux have a clear interest in the capabilities, performance, and reliability of the Linux kernel. Other developer communities focus on different applications and environments that run on Linux, such as Firefox, OpenOffice, GNOME, and KDE. End users, too, can make valuable contributions to the development of Linux. With online communities such as Linux.com, LinuxQuestions, and the many and varied communities hosted by distributions and applications, the Linux user base is often a very vocal, but usually positive advocate and guide for the Linux operating system. The Linux community is not just a online presence. Local groups known as Linux Users Groups (LUGs) often meet to discuss issues regarding the Linux operating system, and provide other local users with free demonstrations, training, technical support, and install-fests.

DEVELOPMENT

Linux is an operating system comprised of many different development languages. A very large percentage of the distributions' code is written in either the C (52.86%) or C++ (25.56%) languages. All of the rest of the code falls into single-digit percentages, with Java, Perl, and Lisp rounding out the top 5 languages. The Linux kernel itself has an even more dominant C presence, with over 95 percent of the kernel's code written in that language. However, other languages make up the kernel as well, making it more heterogeneous than other operating systems. The kernel community has evolved its own distinct way of operating which allows it to function smoothly (and produce a high-quality product) in an environment where thousands of lines of code are being changed every day. This means the Linux kernel development process differs greatly from proprietary development methods.

The kernel's development process may come across as strange and intimidating to new developers, but there are good reasons and solid experience behind it. A developer who does not understand the kernel community's ways (or, worse, who tries to flout or circumvent them) will become very frustrated . The development community, while being helpful to those who are trying to learn, has little time for those who will not listen or who does not care about the development process. While many Linux developers, still use text-based tools such as Emacs or Vim to develop their code, Eclipse, Anjuta, and Netbeans all provide more robust integrated development environments.

Chapter Four: INSTALLING DEBIAN 8

What is Debian

Debian is an all-volunteer organization dedicated to developing free software and promoting the ideals of the Free Software community. The Debian Project began in 1993, when Ian Murdock issued an open invitation to software developers to contribute to a complete and coherent software distribution based on the relatively new Linux kernel. That relatively small band of dedicated enthusiasts, originally funded by the Free Software Foundation and influenced by the GNU philosophy, has grown over the years into an organization of around 1026 *Debian Developers*.

Debian GNU/Linux

The combination of Debian's philosophy, methodology, GNU tools, the Linux kernel, and other important free software, form a unique software distribution called Debian GNU/Linux. This distribution is made up of a large number of software *packages*. Each package in the distribution contains executables, scripts, documentation, and configuration information, and has a *maintainer* who is primarily responsible for keeping the package up-to-date, tracking bug reports, and communicating with the upstream author(s) of the packaged software. The extremely large user base, combined with a bug tracking system ensures that problems are found and fixed quickly. Debian's attention to detail allows them to produce a high-quality, stable, and scalable distribution. Installations can be easily configured to serve many roles, from stripped-down firewalls to scientific desktop workstations to high-end network servers. Debian is especially popular amongst advanced users because of its technical excellence and its deep commitment to the needs and expectations of the Linux community. Debian also introduced many features to Linux that are now commonplace. For example, Debian was the first Linux distribution to include a package management system for the easy installation and removal of software. It was also the first Linux distribution that could be upgraded without requiring re-installation. Debian continues to be a leader in Linux development. Its development process is an example of just how well the Open Source development model can work — even for very complex tasks such as building and maintaining a complete operating system.

The feature that most distinguishes Debian from other Linux distributions is its package management system. These tools gives the administrator of a Debian system complete control over the packages installed, including the ability to install a single package or automatically update the entire operating system. Individual packages can also be protected from being updated. You can even tell the package management system about software you have compiled yourself and what dependencies it fulfills. To protect your system against "Trojan horses" and other malevolent software, Debian's servers verify that uploaded packages come from registered Debian maintainers. Debian packagers also take great care to configure their packages in a secure manner. When security problems in shipped packages do appear, fixes are usually available very quickly.

Installing Debian 8 as a Virtual Machine.

First, you will need to download and install VirtualBox, the Oracle software that allows you to run any OS on... any other OS, as a virtual environment. This procedure is a lot safer than a dual boot: no need to fool around with boot sector or disk partitions, all is virtually created. The counterpart is that the two OS's share your computer resources. To avoid any performance issue, we will choose a lightweight but efficient desktop environment. This book will use the XFCE Debian edition, that you can download using this link below:

https://www.debian.org/CD/torrent-cd/

XFCE is not the newest desktop environment, however it is among the most powerful, lightweight, and customizable, while being easy to use with its classic desktop metaphor.

Imagine an improved version of Windows XP, a great way to get started with Linux.

Create your Virtual System

Once installed, start Virtual Box and follow these steps. We will begin the VM configuration:

- New > Name, Type (debian), Version 64
- General > Advanced > Activate clipboard and Drag'n'drop
- System > check memory, deactivate Floppy, check the nb of CPU (2)
- Display > max video memory, enable 3D acceleration
- Storage > select your Debian ISO under "Controller IDE"
- Shared Folders > choose which folder to share between the systems. We will get back to this function later.

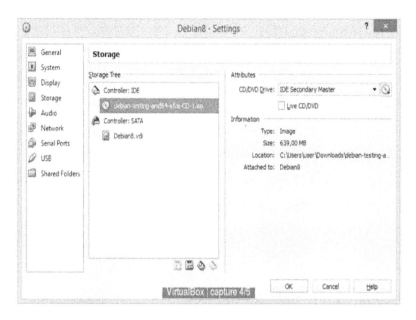

We are now ready to run the distribution installation.

Run Debian installer

Select your virtual machine and click the **'Start'** icon. The Debian graphic installer is straightforward: just follow the steps, when asked enter a root password; create your user (name, username, and password). Once you get to the partitioning, select 'Guided, use entire disk, all in one partition.' If you wish to modify the size of the swap partition, you may select the manual partitioning, or proceed later with Parted, the partitioning utility tool.

Proxy, part #1: select your network mirror. If you need to configure a proxy, use the following syntax in the required field: http://user:pass@host:port/.

Proceed to the installation. Once it has finished, you will have to choose where to install Grub (the boot loader package): because this is a VM install, choose /dev/sda (ata-VBOX_HARDDISK). This would be the tricky part if you were installing on a dual-boot, system so enjoy the comfort of a VM!

Machine View Devices Help

_Debian GNU/Linux installer boot menu

Install
Graphical install
Advanced options   >
Help
Install with speech synthesis

debian
GNU/Linux

Press ENTER to boot or TAB to edit a menu entry

VirtualBox | Install 1/5   CTRL DROITE

debian 8

Configure the package manager

If you need to use a HTTP proxy to access the outside world, enter the proxy information here.
Otherwise, leave this blank.

The proxy information should be given in the standard form of "http://[[user][:pass]@]host[:port]/".
HTTP proxy information (blank for none):

```
http://[user:password]@[host:port]/
```

| Screenshot | VirtualBox | Install 2/5 | Go Back | Continue |

Installing Debian on VirtualBox

Software selection

At the moment, only the core of the system is installed. To tune the system to your needs, you can choose to install one or more of the following predefined collections of software.

Choose software to install:

- ☑ Debian desktop environment
- ☐ ... GNOME
- ☑ ... Xfce
- ☐ ... KDE
- ☐ ... Cinnamon
- ☐ ... MATE
- ☐ ... LXDE
- ☐ web server
- ☑ print server
- ☐ SSH server
- ☑ standard system utilities

Screenshot   VirtualBox | Install 3/5   Continue

Installing Debian on VirtualBox

Install the GRUB boot loader on a hard disk

You need to make the newly installed system bootable, by installing the GRUB boot loader on a bootable device. The usual way to do this is to install GRUB on the master boot record of your first hard drive. If you prefer, you can install GRUB elsewhere on the drive, or to another drive, or even to a floppy.

Device for boot loader installation:

Enter device manually

/dev/sda (ata-VBOX_HARDDISK_VBc08639f2-c96e3459)

Screenshot   VirtualBox | Install 4/5   Go Back   Continue

Installing Debian on VirtualBox

Installing Debian on VirtualBox

Now reboot the VM.

First Boot and Updates

At startup the Grub menu is displayed, stick with the default entry and wait for your system to initialize. At XFCE first start, you will be asked to choose between two panel setups, select the default config.

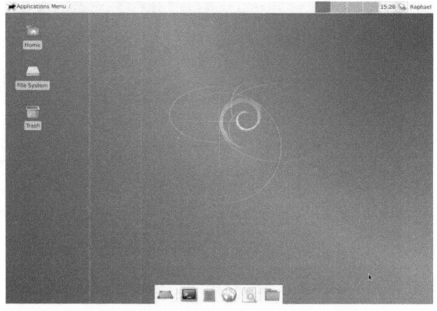

Debian 8 default desktop

Check your time configuration. If incorrect, launch as root a dpkg-reconfigure tzdata and select your country.

Proxy, part #2 (if needed): during install, you entered your proxy address for **apt** connection (repositories connection). It is has been written inside the file /etc/apt/apt.conf, and can be modified any time. I use nano as command line text editor, change at will.

```
[root] $ nano /etc/apt/apt.conf
Acquire::http::Proxy "http://user:password@proxy.address:port/";
```

Now add the proxy setting for the entire system:

```
[root] $ nano /etc/environment
http_proxy=http://user:password@proxy.address:port/
https_proxy=http://user:password@proxy.address:port/
ftp_proxy=http://user:password@proxy.address:port/
```

Congratulations, you are now a confirmed Linux user! Now we can update and install some useful tools, then we will modify the default UI. To use the full capacity of your VM you need to install a complementary VirtualBox extension called **Guest Additions**. To do so, some dependencies are required.

Check your sources, remove the CD entries, add the **contrib** and **non-free** repos:

```
[root] $ nano /etc/apt/sources.list
deb http://ftp.fr.debian.org/debian/ jessie main contrib non-free
deb http://security.debian.org/ jessie/updates main contrib non-free
```

Update your system:

```
[root] $ apt-get update && apt-get dist-upgrade
```

Install the Guest Additions requirements

```
[root] $ apt-get install build-essential module-assistant
[root] $ m-a prepare
```

Insert the Guest Additions CD image (Host + D), go to the root of the mounted drive and execute the program:

```
[root] $ sh ./VBoxLinuxAdditions.run
```

Customizing your System

... to get something that looks a little more modern.

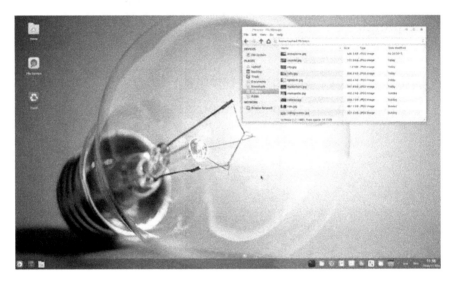

Terminal

The terminal is one of the most useful tools on a Linux system. Spend some time making it pleasant to look at: enable your prompt color ink .bashrc, add your aliases, and enable colors and auto completion in root bash.

```
$ nano ~/.bashrc
```

uncomment the "force_colored_prompt=yes" line

```
[root] $ nano .bashrc
# set a fancy red prompt
PS1='${debian_chroot:+($debian_chroot)}\[33[01;31m\]\u@\h\[33[00
m\]:\[33[01;34m\]\w\[33[00m\] \$ '
# enable auto-completion
if
  [ -f /etc/bash_completion ] && ! shopt -oq posix;
  then . /etc/bash_completion
fi
```

Fonts

Enable **font hinting** in the *Appearance Panel* to get the best font rendering for your system. Settings > Appearance > Fonts > Enable anti-aliasing + Hinting Slight + Sub-pixel order RGB. This should be enough in Jessie, no need to create a fonts.conf file or install the Infinality engine.

Debian XFCE with guest additions, Lightbird GTK and Faience icons

Themes and icons

GTK Themes, windows decoration and iconsets are the most important elements to customizing your desktop. Start with installing some complementary gtk engines that are needed by some themes:

```
[root] $ apt-get install gtk2-engines-murrine gtk2-engines-pixbuf dmz-cursor-theme
```

Install sudo

Debian doesn't come with sudo out of the box, this is a handy little tool for temporarily giving you root access.

```
$ su
$ apt-get install sudo
$ nano /etc/sudoers
```

Add below root ALL=(ALL) ALL:

```
USERNAME ALL=(ALL) NOPASSWD: ALL
```

Replace USERNAME with your username. The NOPASSWD flag removes the requirement to enter a password every time you use sudo. This is *not* a good idea on a production server!

Reboot your machine to make the changes take effect: $ reboot

From now on all operations that require root should be run with the sudo prefix, without having to enter the password each time.

Set up the network

Log in to your new VM using the username and password you chose during installation. We're going to add a network connection to your VM that will allow you too easily SSH into the server.

```
$ sudo nano /etc/network/interfaces
```

Add the following to the end of the file:

```
auto eth1
iface eth1 inet static
address 192.168.56.101
netmask 255.255.255.0
```

Hit CTRL + X, then Y and ENTER to save changes.

Shutdown the VM.

```
$ sudo shutdown -h now
```

At the main Virtual Box screen, hit the Settings button. Then select Network from the list on the left, choose *Adapter 2* from the tabs, check 'Enable Network Adapter' and choose 'Host-only Adapter' from the dropdown, then click OK.

What we have done is set up your VM to use a static IP address. This is a good idea because it allows us to always access our VM using a single IP address/hostname without having to look it up each time we boot.

By default, Virtual Box utilizes the 192.168.56.1 address in your network, and it assigns IP addresses in the 192.168.56.1xx range to all your VMs.

By editing /etc/network/interfaces we told the OS that it should expect a network resource to be available at that address.

Setup your hosts file

Now your server is configured lets add the hostname to your hosts file!

Simply add the following entry into your hosts file. This should be done on your host machine – be it Windows or Mac OS X or Linux, not the VM itself.

```
192.168.56.101    debian-vm
```

Keep in mind that for every domain you setup on your VM, you will need to add it to your hosts file.

Log in via SSH!

Now that you have setup the network adapter in Virtual Box, and added the correct settings to the VM interfaces file, you're ready to actually SSH into your server and begin installing everything! You may be wondering why you need to SSH and not simply use the VM window. The reason I do it this way is that the server does not support copy/paste!

There's a lot of typing ahead and having the ability to simply copy/paste into your terminal is going to speed things up quite a bit!

For SSH on Windows, I use KiTTy. It's an SSH client that adds some nifty features to PuTTY. There is also Poderosa. For Mac/Linux just use the terminal! Since you've already added the correct lines to your hosts file, you can set the address to connect to as debian-vm (or whatever you chose during setup). Make sure to actually start the VM from VirtualBox before attempting to login. Just start it, there is no need to login from the VirtualBox server window.

Installing the basics

First things first, we're going to install the basic necessities, like make, curl, wget, as well as the Apache Server, Mercurial, Git and Subversion:

```
$ sudo apt-get install gcc make wget cron curl libxml2 libxml2-dev libzip-dev \
    libbz2-dev curl libcurl4-openssl-dev libcurl3 libcurl3-gnutls libjpeg62 \
    libjpeg62-dev libpng12-0 libpng12-dev libmcrypt-dev libmcrypt4 libxslt1-dev \
    libxml2-dev apache2 apache2-mpm-prefork apache2-prefork-dev apache2-utils \
    apache2.2-common git mercurial subversion libcupsys2 samba samba-common
```

Edit the new Apache2 config file, `$ sudo nano /etc/apache2/httpd.conf` and add

```
ServerName localhost
```

You now have the Apache server up and running! Just point your browser to http://debian-vm and behold the magic.

Now lets enable Apache's `ModRewrite` module:

```
$ sudo a2enmod rewrite
```

Installing MySQL

We will be installing MySQL 5.1 from repo, as this is the easiest way and works fairly well.

```
$ sudo apt-get install mysql-client-5.1 mysql-server-5.1
```

On the screens asking for a MySQL password, leave it blank and hit Enter. Since this is only for a local server there is no point in setting up a password. Do NOT use a blank password in production environments.

Setting up MySQL

We need to update the IP address that MySQL will listen to for connections by editing the my.cnf file.

```
$ sudo nano /etc/mysql/my.cnf
```

Do a search for `bind-address` (CTRL + W) and change the setting to:

```
bind-address            = 127.0.0.1
bind-address            = 192.168.56.101
```

Now let's grant root MySQL user all permissions:

```
$ mysql -u root
GRANT ALL ON *.* TO 'root'@'%';
exit;
```

and restart the service:

```
$ sudo service mysql restart
```

Chapter Five: INSTALLING CENTOS 7

This is a community-supported distribution derived from sources freely provided to the public by Red Hat for Red Hat Enterprise Linux (RHEL). As such, CentOS Linux aims to be functionally and compatible with RHEL. The CentOS Project mainly changes packages to remove upstream vendor branding and artwork. CentOS Linux is free and free to redistribute. Each CentOS version is maintained for up to 10 years (by means of security updates -- the duration of the support interval by Red Hat has varied over time with respect to Sources released). A new CentOS version is released approximately every 2 years and each CentOS version is periodically updated (roughly every 6 months) to support newer hardware. This results in a secure, low-maintenance, reliable, predictable and reproducible Linux environment.

Installation of CenOS7

Finally, the much-awaited CentOS 7 is out. CentOS (Community Enterprise Operating System) are forked from Red Hat Linux, a Linux Distro fine tuned for servers. You will learn how to install Centos 7 in a few easy steps.

Step 1: Download the ISO Image

To get a copy of CentOS 7 download from the link below:

http://mirror.centos.org/centos/7/

CentOS 7 is only available for 64-bit platforms; currently there is no 32-bit ISO image. This is primarily due to the fact that most production servers are 64-bit.

Step 2: Make a bootable Drive

After you download the ISO image, make a bootable USB drive using Unetbootin. Alternatively, you can burn a DVD using Brasero or your favorite CD/DVD burning software.

Step 3: Begin Installation

To begin installation, click on the Install to Hard Drive icon on the desktop.

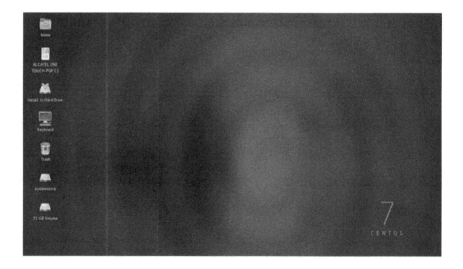

Step 4: Select Language and Keyboard

Select your preferred language.

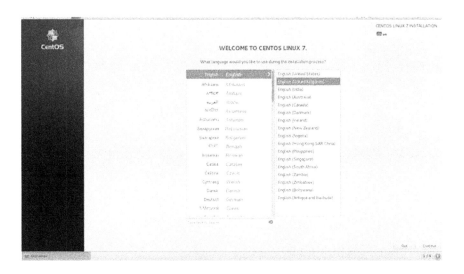

Step 5: Change the Installation Destination

By default, the Anaconda installer will choose automatic partitioning for your hard disk. Click on the INSTALLATION DESTINATION icon to change to custom partitioning.

Select the hard drive where you want to install CentOS 7 and under Other Storage Options, choose 'I will configure partitioning' then click Done.

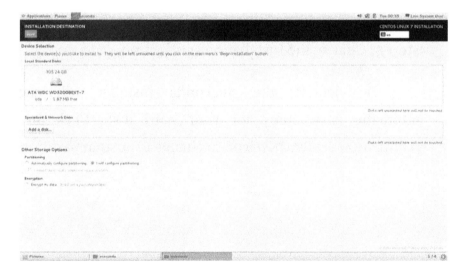

Step 6: Select the Partitioning Scheme

Next, select the partitioning scheme to use for the mountpoints. In this case, choose Standard Partition.

Step 7: Create a Swap Space

You can create a swap space in one of the partitions and set the desired capacity, which is dependent on how much RAM, the system has. Choose the File System for swap space as swap, and select the Reformat option. You can also name your swap space to whatever name you like but a name like swap is more descriptive.

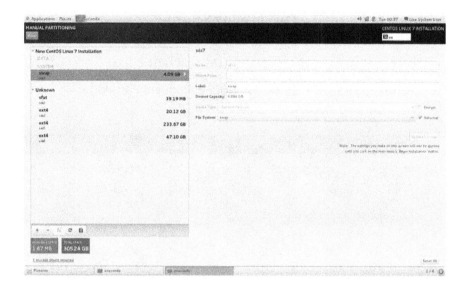

Step 8: Create a Mountpoint

    The next step is to create the mountpoint where the root partition will be installed. Depending on your requirements, you might need to put the boot, home and root partitions on different mountpoints. In this instance, we shall only create one mountpoint /.

Next, set the **Label** and **Desired Capacity** to whatever you wish. A rule of thumb is to use descriptive names for the label especially if the computer is to be managed by different system administrators. Choose the file system as ext4 and select the Reformat option.

Step 9: Accept Changes

After Steps 7 and 8 have successfully completed click on Done button. A prompt window will appear with a summary of the changes that will take place. If you are satisfied with them click Accept Changes.

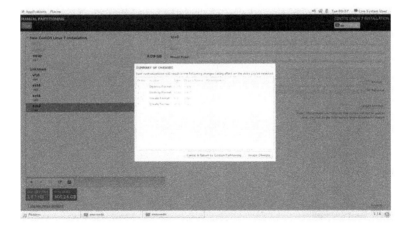

Step 10: Set Date and Time

Click on the Clock icon under the localization menu and select your time zone from the map of the world, then click Done.

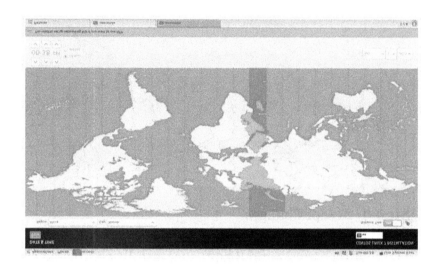

Step 11: Begin Installation

Click on the Begin Installation button.

Installation will begin immediately and as it proceeds you will need to set up a user account as well as the root password.

 Set

Step 12: Set Up Root Password

Click on the ROOT PASSWORD option and enter a password and confirmation of the same then click Done.

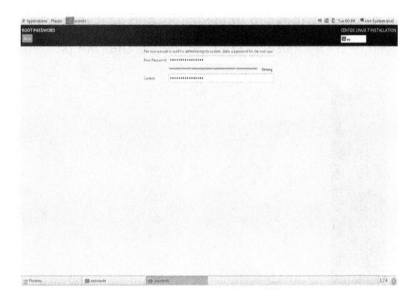

Step 13: Create a User Account

The next step is to create a user account. Enter the details and if this is an administrator account, check Make this user administrator and Require a password to use this account for security purposes.

Step 14: Complete Installation

The installer should finish installing the software and boot loader.

Hopefully, once the install is complete you will get a success message, after which you can click Quit. Now logout from the live system and login to your new installation. Finally, once you login to your CentOS 7 accept the EULA agreement and enjoy!

Change and Set Hostname Command

On a CentOS Linux 7 server, you can use any one of the following tools to manage hostnames:

- hostnamectl: Control the system hostname. This is the recommended method.
- nmtui: Control the system hostname using text user interface (TUI).

- nmcli: Control the system hostname using CLI part of NetworkManager.

Method #1: hostnamectl

Let us see how to use the hostnamectl command.

To verify new settings, enter:

```
# hostnamectl status
```

How do I see the host names?

Sample outputs:

```
Static hostname: server1.cyberciti.biz
   Pretty hostname: Senator Padmé Amidala's Laptop
Transient hostname: r2-d2
         Icon name: computer
           Chassis: n/a
        Machine ID: b5470b10ccfd49ed8e4a3b0e953a53c3
           Boot ID: f79de79e2dac4670bddfe528e826b61f
    Virtualization: oracle
  Operating System: CentOS Linux 7 (Core)
       CPE OS Name: cpe:/o:centos:centos:7
            Kernel: Linux 3.10.0-229.1.2.el7.x86_64
      Architecture: x86_64
```

How do I delete a particular host name?

The syntax is:

```
# hostnamectl set-hostname ""
# hostnamectl set-hostname "" --static
# hostnamectl set-hostname "" -pretty
```

How do I change host name remotely?

Use any of the following syntax:

```
# ssh root@server-ip-here hostnamectl set-hostname server1
```

OR set server1 as host name on a remote server called 192.168.1.42 using ssh:

```
# hostnamectl set-hostname server1 -H root@192.168.1.42
```

Method #2: nmtui

You can set host name using the nmtui command, which has text user interface for new users:

nmtui

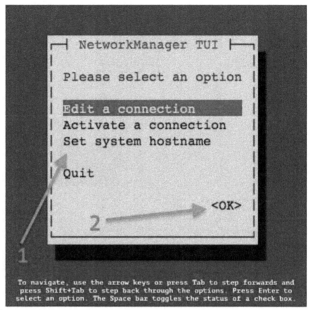

Sample outputs:

Use the **Down** arrow key > select the 'Set system hostname' menu option > Click the OK button:

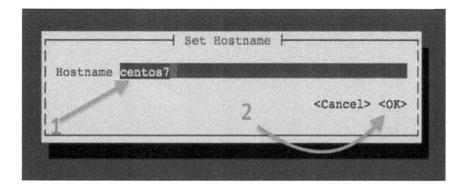

You will see the confirmation box as follows:

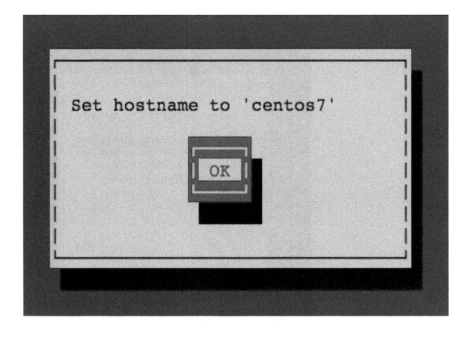

Finally, restart the hostnamed service by typing the following command:

systemctl restart systemd-hostnamed
To verify the changes, enter:
hostnamectl status

Method #3: nmcli

The **nmcli** is a command-line tool for controlling Network Manager and reporting network status.

To view the host name using nmcli:

The syntax is:

```
# nmcli general hostname
```

To set the host name using nmcli:

The syntax is:

```
# nmcli general hostname R2-D2
# nmcli general hostname server42.cyberciti.biz
```

Finally, restart the systemd-hostnamed service:

```
# systemctl restart systemd-hostnamed
```

Chapter Six: LINUX

AND UNIXMAN COMMAND

On Linux and other Unix-like operating systems, *man* is the interface used to view the system's reference manuals.

Syntax

```
man [-C file] [-d] [-D] [--warnings[=warnings]] [-R
encoding] [-L locale]
    [-m system[,...]] [-M path] [-S list] [-e
extension] [-i|-I]
    [--regex|--wildcard] [--names-only] [-a] [-u] [--
no-subpages] [-P pager]
    [-r prompt] [-7] [-E encoding] [--no-hyphenation]
[--no-justification]
    [-p string] [-t] [-T[device]] [-H[browser]] [-
X[dpi]] [-Z]
    [[section] page ...] ...
man -k [apropos options] regexp ...
man -K [-w|-W] [-S list] [-i|-I] [--regex] [section]
term ...
man -f [whatis options] page ...
man -l [-C file] [-d] [-D] [--warnings[=warnings]] [-R
encoding]
    [-L locale] [-P pager] [-r prompt] [-7] [-E
encoding] [-p string] [-t]
    [-T[device]] [-H[browser]] [-X[dpi]] [-Z] file ...
man -w|-W [-C file] [-d] [-D] page ...
man -c [-C file] [-d] [-D] page ...
man [-hV]
```

Description

Man is the system's manual viewer; it can be used to display manual pages, scroll up and down, search for occurrences of specific text, and other useful functions. Each argument given to man is normally the name of a program, utility or function. The pages associated with each of these arguments are then found and displayed. A section number, if provided, will direct man to look only in that section of the manual. The default action is to search in all of the available sections, following a pre-defined order and to show only the first page found, even if pages exist in several sections.

General Options

-h, --help	**Print a help message and exit.**
-V, --version	Display version information and exit.
-C *file*, **--config-file=***file*	Use configuration file *file* rather than the default of ~/.**manpath**.
-d, --debug	Print <u>debugging</u> information.
-D, --default	This option, when used, is normally specified as the first option; it resets**man**'s behaviour to its default. Its use is to reset those options that may have been set in **$MANOPT**. Any options that follow **-D** will have their usual effect.
--warnings[=*warnings***]**	Enable warnings from the **groff** text formatter. This may be used to perform sanity checks on the source text of manual pages. *warnings* is a comma-separated list of warning names; if it is not supplied, the default is "**mac**". See the "**Warnings**" node in the **groff** <u>info</u> page for a list of available warning names.

Main Modes of Operation

-f, --whatis	**Equivalent to the <u>whatis</u> command; displays a short description from the manual page, if available.**
-k, --apropos	Equivalent to the apropos command; Search the short manual page descriptions for keywords and display any matches.
-K, --global-apropos	Search for text in all manual pages. This is a brute-force search, and is likely to take some time; if you can, you should specify a section to reduce the number of pages that need to be searched. Search terms may be simple <u>strings</u> (the default), or <u>regular expressions</u> if the **--regex** option is used.
-l, --local-file	Activate 'local' mode. Format and display local manual files instead of searching through the system's manual collection. Each manual page argument will be interpreted as an <u>nroff</u> source file in the correct format. No <u>cat</u> file is produced. If a dash ('-') is listed as one of the arguments, input will be taken from <u>stdin</u>. When this option is not used, and **man** fails to find the page required, before displaying the error message it attempts to act as if this option was supplied, using the name as a filename and looking for an exact match.
-w, --where, --location	Don't actually display the manual pages; instead print the location(s) of the source **nroff** files that would be formatted.
-W, --where-cat, --	Don't actually display the manual pages, but do print the location(s) of the **cat**files that would be displayed.

location-cat	If **-w** and **-W** are both specified, print both, separated by a space.
-c, --catman	This option is not for general use and should only be used by the **catman**program.
-R *encoding*, **--recode=***encoding*	Instead of formatting the manual page in the usual way, output its source converted to the specified encoding. If you already know the encoding of the source file, you can also use **manconv** directly. However, this option allows you to convert several manual pages to a single encoding without having to explicitly state the encoding of each, provided that they were already installed in a structure similar to a manual page hierarchy.

Finding Manual Pages

-L *locale*, **--locale=***locale*	**man will normally determine your current locale by a call to the C functionsetlocale which checks the values of various environment variables, possibly including $LC_MESSAGES and $LANG. To temporarily override the determined value, use this option to supply a locale string directly to man. Note that it will**

	not take effect until the search for pages actually begins. Output such as the help message will always be displayed in the initially determined locale.
-m *system*[,...], **--systems=***system*[,...]	If this system has access to other operating system's manual pages, they can be accessed using this option. To search for a manual page from (for example) the "NewOS" manual page collection, use the option **-m NewOS**. The system specified can be a combination of comma delimited operating system names. To include a search of the native operating system's manual pages, include the system name **man** in the argument string. This option will override the **$SYSTEM** environment variable.
-M *path*, **--manpath=***path*	Specify an alternate manpath to use. This option overrides the **$MANPATH** environment variable and causes option **-m** to be ignored. A path specified as a manpath must

	be the root of a manual page hierarchy structured into sections as described in the man-db manual (under "The manual page system"). To view manual pages outside such hierarchies, see the -**l** option.
-S *list*, **-s** *list*, **--sections=***list*	*list* is a colon- or comma-separated list of `order specific' manual sections to search. This option overrides the **$MANSECT** environment variable. (The **−s** spelling is for compatibility with System V.)
-e *sub-extension*, **--extension=***sub-extension*	Some systems incorporate large packages of manual pages, such as those that accompany the Tcl package, into the main manual page hierarchy. To get around the problem of having two manual pages with the same name such as exit, the **Tcl** pages were usually all assigned to section **l** (lowercase L). However, it is now possible to put the pages in the correct section, and to assign a specific "extension" to them, in this case, **exit (3tcl)**. Under normal operation, **man** will display **exit** in preference to **exit**

(3tcl). To negotiate this situation and to avoid having to know which section the page you require resides in, it is now possible to give **man** a sub-extension string indicating which package the page must belong to. Using the above example, supplying the option **-e tcl** to **man** will restrict the search to pages having an extension of ***tcl**.

-i, --ignore-case	Ignore case when searching for manual pages. This is the default.
-I, --match-case	Search for manual pages case-sensitively.
--regex	Show all pages with any part of either their names or their descriptions matching each page argument as a regular expression, as with **apropos**. Since there is usually no reasonable way to pick a "best" page when searching for a regular expression, this option implies **-a**.
--wildcard	Show all pages with any part of either their names or their descriptions matching each page argument using shell-style wildcards, as with **apropos --wildcard**. The page

	argument must match the entire name or description, or match on word boundaries in the description. Since there is usually no reasonable way to pick a "best" page when searching for a wildcard, this option implies **-a**.
--names-only	If the **--regex** or **--wildcard** option is used, match only page names, not page descriptions, as with whatis. Otherwise, this option has no effect.
-a, --all	By default, **man** will exit after displaying the most suitable manual page it finds. Using this option forces **man** to display all the manual pages with names that match the search criteria.
-u, --update	This option causes **man** to perform an inode-level consistency check on its database caches to ensure that they are an accurate representation of the filesystem. It will only have a useful effect if **man** is installed with the setuidbit set.
--no-subpages	By default, **man** will try to interpret pairs of manual page names given on the command line as equivalent to a single manual page name containing a

hyphen or an underscore. This supports the common pattern of programs that implement a number of subcommands, allowing them to provide manual pages for each that can be accessed using similar syntax as would be used to invoke the subcommands themselves. For example, the command:

```
man -aw git diff
```

displays the manual page:

```
/usr/share/man/man1/git-diff.1.gz
```

To disable this behavior, use the **--no-subpages** option.

For example:

```
man -aw --no-subpages git diff
```

Will instead show the manual pages for both **git** and **diff**:

```
/usr/share/man/man1/git.1.gz

/usr/share/man/man3/Git.3pm.gz

/usr/share/man/man1/diff.1.gz
```

Controlling Formatted Output

-P *pager*, --pager=*pager*	Specify which output pager to use. By default, man uses pager -s. This option overrides the $MANPAGER environment variable, which in turn overrides the $PAGER environment variable. It is not used in conjunction with -f or -k.
	The value may be a simple command name or a command with arguments, and may use shell quoting (backslashes, single quotes, or double quotes). It may not use pipes to connect multiple commands; if you need that, use a wrapper script, which may take the file to display either as an argument or on standard input.
-r *prompt*, --prompt=*prompt*	If a recent version of less is used as the pager, man will attempt to set its prompt and some

sensible options. The default prompt looks like:

```
Manual page name(sec) line x
```

where name denotes the manual page
name, sec denotes the section it was found under
and x the current line number. This is achieved by
using the $LESS environment variable.

Supplying -r with a string will override this
default. The string may contain the
text $MAN_PN which will be expanded to the
name of the current manual page and its section
name surrounded by "(" and ")". The string used to
produce the default could be expressed as;

```
\ Manual\ page\ \$MAN_PN\ ?ltline\
%lt?L/%L.:


byte\ %bB?s/%s..?\ (END):?pB\
%pB\\%..


(press h for help or q to quit)
```

It is broken into three lines here for the sake of
readability only. For its meaning see the man page
for less.

The shell first evaluates the prompt string. All double quotes, back-quotes and backslashes in the prompt must be escaped by a preceding backslash. The prompt string may end in an escaped $ which may be followed by further options for less. By default, man sets the -ix8 options.

If you want to override man's prompt string processing completely, use the $MANLESS environment variable described below.

-7, --ascii	When viewing a pure ASCII manual page on a 7-bit terminal or terminal emulator, some characters may not display correctly when using the latin1 device description with GNU nroff. This option allows pure ASCII man pages to be displayed in ASCII with the latin1 device. It will not translate any latin1 text. The following table shows the translations performed: some parts of it may only be displayed properly when using GNU nroff's latin1 device. This option is ignored when using options -t, -H, -T, or -Z and may be useless for versions of nroff other than GNU's.
-E *encoding*, **--encoding**=*encodin*	Generate output for a character encoding other than the default. For backward compatibility, encoding may be an nroff device such as ascii,

g	latin1, or utf8 as well as a true character encoding such as UTF-8.
--no-hyphenation, --nh	Normally, nroff will automatically hyphenate text at line breaks even in words that do not contain hyphens, if it is necessary to do lay out thre words on a line without excessive spacing. This option disables automatic hyphenation, so words will only be hyphenated if they already contain hyphens. If you are writing a man page and simply want to prevent nroff from hyphenating a word at an inappropriate point, do not use this option, but consult the nroff documentation instead; for instance, you can put "\%" inside a word to indicate that it may be hyphenated at that point, or put "\%" at the start of a word to prevent it from being hyphenated.
--no-justification, --nj	Normally, nroff will automatically justify text to both margins. This option disables full justification, leaving justified only to the left margin, sometimes called "ragged-right" text.
	If you are writing a man page and simply want to prevent nroff from justifying certain paragraphs, do not use this option, but consult the nroff documentation; for instance, you can use the ".na", ".nf", ".fi", and ".ad" requests to temporarily

	disable adjusting and filling.
-p *string*, **--preprocessor=***string*	Specify the sequence of preprocessors to run before nroff or troff/groff. Not all installations will have a full set of preprocessors. Some of the preprocessors and the letters used to designate them are: eqn (e), grap (g), pic (p), tbl (t), vgrind (v), refer (r). This option overrides the $MANROFFSEQ environment variable. zsoelim is always run as the first preprocessor.
-t, --troff	Use groff -mandoc to format the man page to standard output. This option is not required in conjunction with -H, -T, or -Z.
-T[*device*], **--troff-device**[=*device*]	This option is used to change groff (or possibly troff's) output to be suitable for a device other than the default. It implies -t. Examples include dvi, latin1, ps, utf8, X75 and X100.
-H[*browser*], **--html**[=*browser*]	This option will cause groff to produce HTML output, and will display the output in a web browser. The choice of browser is determined by the optional browser argument if one is provided, by the $BROWSER environment variable, or by a compile-time default if that is unset (usually lynx). This option implies -t, and will only work with GNU troff.
-X[*dpi*], **--**	This option displays the output of groff in a

gxditview[=*dpi*]	graphical window using thegxditview program. The *dpi* (dots per inch) may be 75, 75-12, 100, or 100-12, defaulting to 75; the -12 variants use a 12-point base font. This option implies -T with the X75, X75-12, X100, or X100-12 devices, respectively.
-Z, --ditroff	groff will run troff and then use an appropriate post-processor to produce output suitable for the chosen device. If groff -mandoc is groff, this option is passed to groff and will suppress the use of a post-processor. It implies -t.

Section Numbers

The section numbers of the manual are listed below. While reading documentation, if you see a command name followed by a number in parentheses, the number refers to one of these sections. For example, man is the documentation of man found in section number1. Some commands may have documentation in more than one section, so the numbers after the command name may direct you to the correct section to find a specific type of information.

The section numbers, and the topics they cover, are as follows:

section #	Topic

1	Executable programs or shell commands
2	System calls (functions provided by the kernel)
3	Library calls (functions within program libraries)
4	Special files (usually found in /dev)
5	File formats and conventions eg /etc/passwd
6	Games
7	Miscellaneous (including macro packages and conventions), e.g. man, groff
8	System administration commands (usually only for root)
9	Kernel routines [Non standard]

Exit Status

When it terminates, **man** will return one of the following exit status:

0	**Returned upon successful program execution.**
1	Returned if there was a usage, syntax, or configuration file error.
2	Returned if there was an operational error.
3	Returned if a child process returned a non-zero exit status.

16 Returned if one or more of the pages, files, or keywords searched for did not exist or was not matched.

Environment

man makes use of the following environment variables:

MANPATH	**If $MANPATH is set, its value is used as the path to search for manual pages.**
MANROFFOPT	The contents of **$MANROFFOPT** are added to the command line every time **man** invokes the formatter (nroff, troff, or **groff**).
MANROFFSEQ	If **$MANROFFSEQ** is set, its value is used to determine the set of preprocessors to pass each manual page through. The default preprocessor list is system-dependent.
MANSECT	If **$MANSECT** is set, its value is a colon-delimited list of sections and it is used to determine which man sections to search and in what order.

MANPAGER, PAGER	If **$MANPAGER** or **$PAGER** is set (**$MANPAGER** is used in preference), its value is used as the name of the program used to display the man page. By default, **pager -s** is used. The value may be a simple command name or a command with arguments, and may use shell quoting (backslashes, single quotes, or double quotes). It may not use pipes to connect multiple commands; if you need that, use a wrapper script, which may take the file to display either as an argument or on standard input.
MANLESS	If **$MANLESS** is set, man will not perform any of its usual processing to set up a prompt string for the less pager. Instead, the value of **$MANLESS** will be copied verbatim into **$LESS**. For example, if you want to set the prompt string unconditionally to "my prompt string",

	set **$MANLESS** to '**-Psmy prompt string**'.
BROWSER	If **$BROWSER** is set, its value is a colon-delimited list of commands, each of which in turn is used to try to start a web browser for **man --html**. In each command, **%s** is replaced by a filename containing the HTML output from **groff**, **%%** is replaced by a single percent sign (**%**), and **%c** is replaced by a colon (**:**).
SYSTEM	If **$SYSTEM** is set, it will have the same effect as if it had been specified as the argument to the **-m** option.
MANOPT	If **$MANOPT** is set, it will be parsed prior to **man**s command line and is expected to be in a similar format. As all of the other man specific environment variables can be expressed as command line options, and are thus candidates for being included

	in **$MANOPT** it is expected that they will become obsolete. Note: all spaces that should be interpreted as part of an option's argument must be escaped (preceded with a backslash).
MANWIDTH	If **$MANWIDTH** is set, its value is used as the line length for which manual pages should be formatted. If it is not set, manual pages will be formatted with a line length appropriate to the current terminal (using an **ioctl** if available, the value of **$COLUMNS**, or falling back to 80 characters if neither is available). **cat** pages will only be saved when the default formatting can be used, that is when the terminal line length is between 66 and 80 characters.
MAN_KEEP_FORMATTING	Normally, when output is not being directed to a terminal (such as to a file or a pipe), formatting characters are

	discarded to make it easier to read the result without special tools. However, if **$MAN_KEEP_FORMATTING** is set to any non-empty value, these formatting characters are retained. This may be useful for wrappers around **man** that can interpret formatting characters.
MAN_KEEP_STDERR	Normally, when output is being directed to a terminal (usually a pager), any error output from the command used to produce formatted versions of man pages is discarded to avoid interfering with the pager's display. Programs such as **groff** often produce relatively minor error messages about typographical problems such as poor alignment, which are unsightly and generally confusing when displayed along with the man page. However, you might want to see them anyway, so if **$MAN_KEEP_STDERR** i

	s set to a non-empty value, error output will be displayed as usual.
LANG, LC_MESSAGES	Depending on the system and implementation, either or both of **$LANG** and **$LC_MESSAGES** will be interrogated for the current message locale, **man** will display its messages in that locale (if available).

Files

These files are used by **man**:

/etc/manpath.config	The **man-db** configuration file.
/usr/share/man	A global manual page

	hierarchy.
/usr/share/man/index.(bt|db|dir|pag)	A traditional global index database cache.
/var/cache/man/index.(bt|db|dir|pag)	An FHS compliant global index database cache.

Examples

```
man man
```

View the man page for the man command.

```
man --nh --nj man
```

Chapter Seven: LINUX

DIRECTORY COMMAND

Linux or UNIX-like systems use the ls command to list files and directories. However, ls does not have an option to list only directories. You can use combination of ls and grep to list directory names only. You can use the find command too. In this quick tutorial, you will learn how to list only directories in Linux or UNIX.

List all directories in Unix

Type the following command:

$ ls -l | grep `^d'
ls -l | egrep `^d'

Try the following ls command to list directories in the current directory:

$ ls -d */

```
desktop01:- vivek$ pwd
/Users/vivek
desktop01:- vivek$ ls -d */
Accounting/              Pictures/              music/
Applications/            Public/                old.data/
Books/                   VirtualBox VMs/        perl5/
Desktop/                 backups/               r/
Documents/               bin/                   securebackups.realdata/
Downloads/               demo/                  usb/
Library/                 dev/                   yuicompressor/
Movies/                  google-cloud-sdk/
Music/                   isos/
desktop01:- vivek$ find . -maxdepth 1 -type d
.                                          Includes
./.Trash                                  hidden dirs names
./.ansible                                too with the find
./.bashish                                    command
./.cache
./.config
./.cpan
./.cups
```

sample outputs

List only files in Unix

Type the following command:

```
$ ls -l | egrep -v '^d'
$ ls -l | egrep -v '^d'
```

The grep command is used to searches input. It will filter out directory names by matching first character 'd'. To reverse the effect i.e. just to display files you need to pass the -v option. It inverts the sense of matching, to select non-matching lines.

Task: Create aliases to save time

You can create two aliases to list only directories and files.
```
alias lf="ls -l | egrep -v '^d'"
```

```
alias ldir="ls -l | egrep '^d'"
```

Put above two aliases in your bash shell startup file:

```
$ cd
$ vi .bash_profile
```

Append two lines:

```
alias lf="ls -l | egrep -v '^d'"
alias ldir="ls -l | egrep '^d'"
```

Save and close the file.

Now just type lf - to list files and ldir - to list directories only:

```
$ cd /etc
$ lf
```

Sample output:

```
-rw-r--r--    1 root root        2149 2006-09-04 23:25
adduser.conf
-rw-r--r--    1 root root          44 2006-09-29 05:11
adjtime
-rw-r--r--    1 root root         197 2006-09-04 23:48
aliases
-rw-------    1 root root         144 2002-01-18 13:43
at.deny
-rw-r--r--    1 root root         162 2006-09-22 23:24
aumixrc
-rw-r--r--    1 root root          28 2006-09-22 23:24
aumixrc1
```

List directory names only:

```
$ cd /etc
$ ldir
```

Sample output:

```
drwxr-xr-x    4 root root        4096 2006-09-22 16:41 alsa
```

```
drwxr-xr-x    2 root root        4096 2006-09-20 20:59
alternatives
drwxr-xr-x    6 root root        4096 2006-09-22 16:41 apm
drwxr-xr-x    3 root root        4096 2006-09-07 02:51 apt
drwxr-xr-x    2 root root        4096 2006-09-08 01:46
bash_completion.d
```
Use find command to list either files or directories

The find command can be used as follows: to list all directories in /nas, enter:

```
find /nas -type d
find /nas -type d -ls
find . -type d -ls
```

Sample output:

```
1070785    8 drwxrwxrwt  8 root     root        4096
Jul  5 07:12 .
1070797    8 drwx------  2 root     root        4096
Jul  4 07:22 ./orbit-root
1070843    8 drwxr-xr-x  2 root     root        4096
Jun 16 18:55 ./w
1070789    8 drwxr-xr-x 10 root     root        4096
Jun 17 14:54 ./b
1071340    8 drwxr-xr-x  2 root     root        4096
Jun 16 18:55 ./b/init.d
1071581    8 drwxr-xr-x  3 root     root        4096
Jun 16 18:55 ./b/bind
1071584    8 drwxr-xr-x  2 root     root        4096
Jun 16 18:55 ./b/bind/bak
1071617    8 drwxr-xr-x  2 root     root        4096
Jun 16 18:55 ./b/fw
1071628    8 drwxr-xr-x  8 root     root        4096
Jun 16 18:55 ./b/scripts
```

Chapter Eight: WORKING WITH FILES

This chapter will first describe general characteristics of Unix commands. It will then discuss commands, which are commonly used to create and manipulate files. A summary of some of the most commonly used UNIX commands is presented in Command Comparisons.

UNIX File Names

It is important to understand the rules for creating UNIX files: UNIX is case sensitive! For example, "fileName" is different from "filename." It is recommended that you limit names to the alphabetic characters, numbers, underscore (_), and dot (.). Dots (.) used in UNIX filenames are simply characters and not delimiters between filename components; you may include more than one dot in a filename. Including a dot as the first character of a filename makes the file invisible (hidden) to the normal ls command; use the -a flag of the ls command to display hidden files. Although many systems will allow more, the recommended length is 14 characters per file name. Unix shells typically include several important wildcard characters. The asterisk (*) is used to match 0 or more character (e.g., abc* will match any file beginning with the letters abc), the question mark (?) is used to match any single character, and the left ([) and right (]) square brackets are used to enclose a string of characters, any one of which is to match. Execute the following commands and observe the results:

```
ls  m*
ls  *.f
ls  *.?
ls  [a-d]*
```

Notes for PC users: Unix uses forward slashes (/) instead of backslashes (\ ) for directories

Looking at the Contents of Files

You can examine the contents of files using a variety of commands. cat, more, pg, head,   and tail are   described here. Of course, you can always use an editor; to use vi in "read-only" mode to examine the contents of the file "argtest", enter:

```
vi   -R    argtest
```

You can now use the standard vi commands to move through the file; however, you will not be able to make any changes to the contents of the file. This option is useful when you simply want to look at a file and want to guarantee that you make no changes while doing so.

Use the vi "" command to exit from the file.

Cat Command

`cat` is a utility used to conCATenate files. Thus, it can be used to join files together, but it is perhaps more commonly used to display the contents of a file on the screen.

Observe the output produced by each of the following commands:

```
cd;      cd  xmp
cat           cars
cat  -vet  cars
cat  -n     cars
```

The semicolon (;) in the first line of this example is a command separator which enables entry of more than one command on a line. When the `<Return>` key is pressed following this line, the command cd is issued which changes to your home directory. Then the command "`cd xmp`" is issued to change into the subdirectory "xmp." Entering this line is equivalent to having entered these commands sequentially on separate lines. These two commands are included in the example to guarantee that you are in the subdirectory containing "cars" and the other example files. You need not enter these commands if you are already in the "xmp" directory created when you copied the example file.

The "-vet" option enables display of tab, end-of-line, and other non-printable characters within a file; the "-n" option numbers each line as it is displayed.

You can also use the cat command to join files together:

```
cat    page1
cat    page2
cat    page1   page2 > document
cat    document
```

Note: If the file "document" had previously existed, it will be replaced by the contents of files "page1" and "page2."

Cautions to using the cat command: The cat command should only be used with "text" files; it should not be used to display the contents of binary (e.g., compiled C or FORTRAN programs). Unpredictable results may occur, including the termination of your logon session. Use the command "file *" to display the characteristics of files within a directory prior to using the cat command with any unknown file. You can use the od(enter "man od" for details on use of Octal Dump) command to display the contents of non-text files. For example, to display the contents of "a.out" in both hexadecimal and character representation, enter:

```
od   -xc   a.out
```

Warning: cat (and other Unix commands) can destroy files if not used correctly. For example, as illustrated in the Sobell book, the `cat` (also `cp` and `mv`) command can overwrite and thus destroy files. Observe the results of the following command:

```
cat  letter page1 >  letter
```

Typically, UNIX does not return a message when a command executes successfully. Here the UNIX operating system will attempt to complete the requested command by first initializing the file "letter" and then writing the current contents of "letter" (now nothing) and "page1" into this file. Since "letter" has been reinitialized and is also named as a source file, an error diagnostic is generated. Part of the UNIX philosophy is "No news is good news." Thus, the appearance of a message is a warning that the command was not completed successfully.

Now use the "`cat`" command to individually examine the contents of the files "letter" and "page1." Observe that the file "letter" does not contain the original contents of the files "letter" and "page1" as was intended.

Use the following command to restore the original file "letter":

```
cp  ~aixstu00/xmp/letter .
```

More Command

You may type or browse files using the more command. The "more" command is useful when examining a large file as it displays the file contents one page at a time, allowing each page to be examined at will. As with the man command, you must press the space bar to proceed to the next screen of the file. On many systems, pressing the <b> key will enable you to page backwards in the file. To terminate more at any time, press <q>.

To examine a file with the more command, simply enter:

```
more   file_name
```

The man command uses the more command to display the manual pages; thus, the commands you are familiar with using man will also work with more.

Not all Unix systems include the more command; some implement the pg command instead. VTAIX includes both the more and pg commands. When using the pg command, press <Return> to page down through a file instead of using the space bar.

Observe the results of entering the following commands:

```
more   argtest


pg     argtest
```

Head Command

The head command is used to display the first few lines of a file. This command can be useful when you wish to look for specific information, in the beginning of the file. For example, enter:

```
head  argtest
```

Tail Command

The `tail` command is used to display the last lines of a file. This command can be useful to monitor the status of a program, which appends output to the end of a file. For example, enter:

```
tail  argtest
```

Copying, Erasing, Renaming

Warning: The typical Unix operating system provides no 'unerase' or 'undelete' command. If you mistakenly delete a file you are dependent upon the backups you or the system administrator have maintained in order to recover the file. You need to be careful when using commands like copy and move, which may result in overwriting existing files. If you are using the C or Korn Shell, you can create a command <u>alias</u> , which will prompt you for verification before overwriting files with these commands.

Copying Files

The cp command is used to copy a file or group of files. You have already seen an example application of the cp command when you copied the sample files to your userid. Now let's make a copy of one of these files. Recall that you can obtain a listing of the files in the current directory using the ls command. Observe the results from the following commands:

```
ls   1*
cp   letter   letter.2
ls   1*
```

Note: Unlike many other operating systems, such as PC/DOS, you must specify the target with the copy command; it does not assume the current directory if no "copy-to" target is specified.

Erasing Files

Unix uses the command rm (ReMove) to delete unwanted files. To remove the file "letter.2" which we have just created, enter:

```
rm   letter.2
```

Enter the command "ls 1*" to display a list of all files beginning with the letter "l." Note that letter.2 is no longer present in the current directory. The remove command can be used with wildcards in filenames; however, this can be dangerous as you might end up erasing files you had wanted to keep. It is recommended that you use the "-i" (interactive) option of rm for wildcard deletes — you will then be prompted to respond with a "y" or "Y" for each file you wish to delete.

Renaming a File

The typical Unix operating system utilities do not include a rename command; however, we can use the mv (MoVe) command (see for additional uses of this command) to "move" Working with Directories) a file from one name to another. Observe the results of the following commands:

```
ls    [d,l]*
mv    letter   document
ls    [d,l]*
mv    document letter
ls    [d,l]*
```

Note: The first mv command overwrites the file "document" which you had created in an earlier exercise by concatenating "page1" and "page2." No warning is issued when the mv command is used to move a file into the name of an existing file. If you would like to be prompted for confirmation if the mv command were to overwrite an existing file, use the "-i" (interactive) option of the mv command, e.g.:

```
mv   -i   page1   letter
```

You will now be told that the file "letter" already exists and you will be asked if you wish to proceed with the `mv` command. Answer anything but "`y`" or "`Y`" and the file "letter" will not be overwritten.

Using the Command Line

The command interpreter (shell) provides the mechanism by which input commands are interpreted and passed to the Unix kernel or other programs for processing. Observe the results of entering the following commands:

```
./filesize
./hobbit
./add2
ls -F
```

Observe that "filesize" is an executable shell script, which displays the size of files. Also note that "./hobbit" and "./add2" generate error diagnostics as there is no command or file with the name "hobbit" and the file "add2" lacks execute permission.

Standard Input and Standard Output

As you have can see, Unix expects standard input to come from the keyboard, e.g., enter:

```
cat
my_text
```

```
<Ctrl-D>
```

Standard output is typically displayed on the terminal screen, e.g., enter:

```
cat cars
```

Standard error (a listing of program execution error diagnostics) is typically displayed on the terminal screen, e.g., enter:

```
ls xyzpqrz
```

Redirection

As illustrated above, many Unix commands read from standard input (typically the keyboard) and write to standard output (typically the terminal screen). The redirection operators enable you to read input from a file (<) or write program output to a file (>). When output is redirected to a file, the program output replaces the original contents of the file if it already exists; to add program output to the end of an existing file, use the append redirection operator (>>).

Observe the results of the following command:

```
./a.out
```

You will be prompted to enter a Fahrenheit temperature. After entering a numeric value, a message will be displayed on the screen informing you of the equivalent Centigrade temperature. In this example, you entered a numeric value as standard input via the keyboard and the output of the program was displayed on the terminal screen.

In the next example, you will read data from a file and have the result displayed on the screen (standard output):

```
cat   data.in
./a.out   <   data.in
```

Now you will read from standard input (keyboard) and write to a file:

```
./a.out   >   data.two
35
cat   data.two
```

Now read from standard input and append the result to the existing file:

```
./a.out   <   data.in   >>   data.two
```

As another example of redirection, observe the result of the following two commands:

```
ls   -la   /etc   >   temp
```

```
more   temp
```

Here we have redirected the output of the `ls` command to the file "temp" and then used the `more` command to display the contents of this file a page at a time. In the next section, we will see how the use of pipes could simplify this operation.

Using Pipes and Filters

A filter is a Unix program, which accepts input from standard input and places its output in standard output. Filters add power to the UNIX system as programs can be written to use the output of another program as input and create output, which can be used by yet another program. A pipe (indicated by the symbol "|" — vertical bar) is used between UNIX commands to indicate that the output from the first is to be used as input by the second. Compare the output from the following two commands:

```
ls -la /etc
ls -la /etc | more
```

The first command displays of all the files in the in the "/etc" directory in long format. It is difficult to make use of this information since it scrolls rapidly across the screen. In the second line, the results of the `ls` command are piped into the `more` command. We can now examine this information one screen at a time and can even back up to a prior screen of information if we wish to. As you became more familiar with UNIX, you will find that piping output to the `more` command can be very useful in a variety of applications.

The `sort` command can be used to sort the lines in a file in a desired order. Now enter the following commands and observe the results:

```
who
sort cars
who  |  sort
```

The `who` command displays a list of users currently logged onto the system the `sort` command enables us to sort the information. The second command sorts the lines in the file cars alphabetically by first field and displays the result in standard output. The third command illustrates how the result of the `who` command can be passed to the sort command prior to being displayed. The result is a listing of logged on users in alphabetical order.

The following example uses the "`awk`" and "`sort`" commands to select and reorganize the output generated by the "`ls`" command:

```
ls -l | awk '/:/ {print $5,$9}' | sort -nr
```

Note: Curly braces do not necessarily display correctly on all output devices. In the above example, there should be a left curly brace in front of the word print and a right curly brace following the number 9.

Observe that the output displays the filesize and filename in decreasing order of size. Here the ls command first generates a "long" listing of the files in the current directory, which is piped to the "awk" utility, whose output is then piped to the "sort" command.

"awk" is a powerful utility which processes one or more program lines to find patterns within a file and perform selective actions based on what is found. Slash (/) characters are used as delimiters around the pattern to be matched and the action to be taken is enclosed in curly braces. If no pattern is specified, all lines in the file are processed and if no action is specified, all lines matching the specified pattern are output. Since a colon (:) is used here, all lines containing file information (the time column corresponding to each file contains a colon) are selected and the information contained in the 5th and 9th columns are output to the sort command.

Note: If the ls command on your system does not include a column listing group membership, use {print $4,$8} instead of the "print" command option of awk listed above.

Here the "`sort`" command options "`-nr`" specify that the output from "`awk`" be sorted in reverse numeric order, i.e., from largest to smallest.

The preceding command is somewhat complex and it is easy to make a mistake in entering it. If this were a command you would use frequently, we could include it in a <u>shell script</u> as in sample file "filesize". To use this shell script, simply enter the command:

```
./filesize
     or
 sh   filesize
```

If you examine the contents of this file with the `cat` or `vi` commands, you will see that it contains nothing more the piping of the `ls` command to `awk` and then piping the output to `sort`.

The `tee` utility is used to send output to both a file and the screen:

```
who | tee who.out | sort


cat who.out
```

Here you should have observed that a list of logged on users was displayed on the screen in alphabetical order and that the file "who.out" contained an unsorted listing of the same userids.

Some Additional File Handling Commands

Word Count

The command wc displays the number of lines, words, and characters in a file.

To display the number of lines, words, and characters in the file file_name, enter:

```
wc file_name
```

Comparing the Contents of Two Files: the cmp and diff Commands

The cmp and diff commands are used to compare files; the "comp" command is not used to compare files, but to "compose a message."

The cmp command can be used for both binary and text files. It indicates the location (byte and line) where the first difference between the two files appears.

The diff command can be used to compare text files and its output shows the lines which are different in the two files: a less than sign ("<") appears in front of lines from the first file which differ from those in the second file, a greater than symbol (">") precedes lines from the second file. Matching lines are not displayed.

Observe the results of the following commands:

```
cmp     page1   page2
diff    page1   page2
```

Lines 1 and 2 of these two files are identical, lines 3 differ by one character, and page one contains a blank line following line three, while page2 does not.

Chapter Nine:

NAVIGATION AND FILE MANAGEMENT

If you do not have much experience working with Linux systems, you may be overwhelmed by the prospect of controlling an operating system from the command line. In this book, we will attempt to get you up to speed with the basics.

Prerequisites and Goals

In order to follow along with this book, you will need to have access to a Linux server. You will also want to have a basic understanding of how the terminal works and what Linux commands look like. This book covers terminal basics, so you should check it out if you are new to using terminals. All of the material in this book can be accomplished with a regular, non-root (non-administrative) user account. You can learn how to configure this type of user account by following your distribution's initial server setup guide (Ubuntu 14.04, CentOS 7). When you are ready to begin, connect to your Linux server using SSH and continue below.

Navigation and Exploration

The most fundamental skills you need to master are navigating the filesystem. We will discuss the tools that allow you to do this in this section.

Finding where you are with the "pwd" command

When you log onto your server, you are typically dropped into your user accounts **home directory**. A home directory is the directory set aside for your account to store files and create directories. It is the location in the filesystem where you have full dominion. To find out where your home directory is in relationship to the rest of the filesystem, you can use the `pwd` command. This command displays the directory that we are currently in:

```
pwd
```

You should get back some information that looks like this:

```
/home/demo
```

The home directory is named after the user account, so the above example is what the value would be if you were logged into the server with an account called `demo`. This directory is within a directory called `/home`, which is itself within the top-level directory, which is called "root" represented by a single slash "/".

Looking at the Contents of Directories with "ls"

Now that you know how to display the directory that you are in, we can show you how to look at the contents of a directory.

Currently, your home directory does contain much, so we will go to another, more populated directory to explore. Type the following command in your terminal to change directory (we will explain the details of moving directories in the next section). Afterward, we will use pwd to confirm that we successfully moved:

```
cd /usr/share
pwd
/usr/share
```

Now that we are in a new directory, let us look at what's inside. To do this, we can use the ls command:

```
ls
adduser             groff
pam-configs
applications        grub
perl
apport              grub-gfxpayload-lists
perl5
apps                hal
pixmaps
```

```
apt                  i18n
pkgconfig
aptitude             icons
polkit-1
apt-xapian-index     info
popularity-contest
. . .
```

As you can see, there are *many* items in this directory. We can add some optional flags to the command to modify the default behavior. For instance, to list all of the contents in an extended form, we can use the -l flag (for "long" output):

```
ls -l
total 440
drwxr-xr-x    2 root root   4096 Apr 17  2014 adduser
drwxr-xr-x    2 root root   4096 Sep 24 19:11
applications
drwxr-xr-x    6 root root   4096 Oct  9 18:16 apport
drwxr-xr-x    3 root root   4096 Apr 17  2014 apps
drwxr-xr-x    2 root root   4096 Oct  9 18:15 apt
drwxr-xr-x    2 root root   4096 Apr 17  2014 aptitude
drwxr-xr-x    4 root root   4096 Apr 17  2014 apt-
xapian-index
drwxr-xr-x    2 root root   4096 Apr 17  2014 awk
. . .
```

This view gives us plenty of information, most of which looks rather unusual. The first block describes the file type (if the first column is a "d" the item is a directory, if it is a "-", it is a normal file) and permissions. Each subsequent column, separated by white space, describes the number of hard links, the owner, group owner, item size, last modification time, and the name of the item. We will describe some of these at another time, but for now, just know that you can view this information with the `-l` flag of `ls`.

To get a listing of all files, including *hidden* files and directories, you can add the `-a` flag. Since there are no real hidden files in the `/usr/share` directory, let's go back to our home directory and try that command. You can get back to the home directory by typing `cd` with no arguments:

```
cd
ls -a
.   ..   .bash_logout   .bashrc   .profile
```

As you can see, there are three hidden files in this demonstration, along with `.` and `..`, which are special indicators. You will find that often, configuration files are stored as hidden files.

The dot and double dot entries, are built-in methods of referring to related directories. The single dot indicates the current directory, and the double dot indicates this directory's parent directory. This will come in handy in the next section.

Moving Around the Filesystem with "cd"

We have already changed directories twice to demonstrate some properties of `ls`. Let's take a better look at the command here.

Begin by going back to the `/usr/share` directory by typing this:

```
cd /usr/share
```

This is an example of changing a directory by giving an absolute path. In Linux, every file and directory is under the top-most directory, which is called the "root" directory, but referred to by a single leading slash "/". An absolute path indicates the location of a directory in relation to this top-level directory. This lets us refer to directories in an unambiguous way from any place in the filesystem. Every absolute path must begin with a slash.

The alternative is to use relative paths. Relative paths refer to directories in relation to the *current* directory. For directories close to the current directory in the hierarchy, this is usually easier and shorter. Any directory within the current directory can be referenced by name without a leading slash. We can change to the `locale` directory within `/usr/share` from our current location by typing:

```
cd locale
```

We can likewise change multiple directory levels with relative paths by providing the portion of the path that comes after the current directory's path. From here, we can get to the `LC_MESSAGES` directory within the `en` directory by typing:

```
cd en/LC_MESSAGES
```

To move up one directory level, we use the special double dot indicator we talked about earlier. For instance, we are now in the `/usr/share/locale/en/LC_MESSAGES` directory. To move up one level, we can type:

```
cd ..
```

This takes us to the `/usr/share/locale/en` directory.

A shortcut that you saw earlier that will always take you back to your home directory is to use `cd` without providing a directory:

```
cd
pwd
/home/demo
```

Viewing Files

In the last section, we learned how to navigate the filesystem. In this section, we will discuss different ways to view files. In contrast to some operating systems, Linux and other Unix-like operating systems rely on plain text files for vast portions of the system. The main way that we will view files is with the `less` command. This is what we call a "pager," because it allows us to scroll through pages of a file. While the previous commands immediately executed and returned you to the command line, `less` is an application that will continue to run and occupy the screen until you exit.

We will open the `/etc/services` file, which is a configuration file that contains the systems services information:

```
less /etc/services
```

The file will be opened in `less`, allowing you to see the portion of the document that fits in the terminal window:

```
# Network services, Internet style
#
# Note that it is presently the policy of IANA to
assign a single well-known
# port number for both TCP and UDP; hence,
officially ports have two entries
# even if the protocol doesn't support UDP
operations.
#
# Updated from http://www.iana.org/assignments/port-
numbers and other
```

```
# sources like
http://www.freebsd.org/cgi/cvsweb.cgi/src/etc/servic
es .
# New ports will be added on request if they have
been officially assigned
# by IANA and used in the real-world or are needed
by a debian package.
# If you need a huge list of used numbers please
install the nmap package.

tcpmux            1/tcp                              #
TCP port service multiplexer
echo              7/tcp
. . .
```

To scroll, you can use the up and down arrow keys on your keyboard. To page down one whole screens-worth of information, you can use either the space bar, the "Page Down" button on your keyboard, or the CTRL-f shortcut.

To scroll back up, you can use either the "Page Up" button, or the CTRL-b keyboard shortcut. To search for some text in the document, you can type a forward slash "/" followed by the search term. For instance, to search for "mail", we would type: /mail This will search forward through the document and stop at the first result. To get to another result, you can type the lower-case n key:

```
n
```

To move backwards to the previous result, use a capital N instead:

N

When you wish to exit the less program, you can type q to quit:

q

While we focused on the less tool in this section, there are many other ways of viewing a file. The cat command displays a file's contents and returns you to the prompt immediately. The head command, by default, shows the first 10 lines of a file. Likewise, the tail command shows the last 10 lines. These commands display file contents in a way that is useful for "piping" to other programs. We will discuss this concept in a future guide.

Feel free to see how these commands display the /etc/services file differently.

File and Directory Manipulation

We learned in the last section how to view a file. In this section, we will demonstrate how to create and manipulate files and directories.

Create a File with "touch"

Many commands and programs can create files. The most basic method of creating a file is with the `touch` command. This will create an empty file using the name and location specified.

First, we should make sure we are in our home directory, since this is a location where we have permission to save files. Then, we can create a file called `file1` by typing:

```
cd
touch file1
```

Now, if we view the files in our directory, we can see our newly created file:

```
ls
file1
```

If we use this command on an existing file, the command simply updates the data our filesystem stores on the time when the file was last accessed and modified.

We can also create multiple files at the same time. We can use absolute paths as well. For instance, if our user account is called `demo`, we could type:

```
touch /home/demo/file2 /home/demo/file3
ls
file1   file2   file3
```

Create a Directory with "mkdir"

Similar to the `touch` command, the `mkdir` command allows us to create empty directories.

For instance, to create a directory within our home directory called `test`, we could type:

```
cd
mkdir test
```

We can make a directory *within* the `test` directory called `example` by typing:

```
mkdir test/example
```

For the above command to work, the `test` directory must already exist. To tell `mkdir` that it should create any directories necessary to construct a given directory path, you can use the `-p` option. This allows you to create nested directories in one step. We can create a directory structure that looks like `some/other/directories` by typing:

```
mkdir -p some/other/directories
```

The command will make the `some` directory first, then it will create the `other` directory in the `some` directory. Finally, it will create the `directories` directory in the `other` directory.

Moving and Renaming Files and Directories with "mv"

We can move a file to a new location using the `mv` command. For instance, we can move `file1` into the `test` directory by typing:

```
mv file1 test
```

For this command, we list all items that we want to move, with the location to move them to. We can move that file *back* to our home directory by using the special dot reference to refer to our current directory. We should make sure we are in our home directory, and then execute the command:

```
cd
mv test/file1 .
```

This may seem unintuitive at first, but the `mv` command is also used to *rename* files and directories. In essence, moving and renaming are both just adjusting the location and name for an existing item.

So to rename the `test` directory to `testing`, we could type:

```
mv test testing
```

Note: It is important to realize that your Linux system will not prevent you from certain destructive actions. If you are renaming a file and choose a name that *already* exists, the previous file will be **overwritten** by the file you are moving. There is no way to recover the previous file if you accidentally overwrite it.

Copying Files and Directories with "cp"

With the `mv` command, we could move or rename a file or directory, but we could not duplicate it. The `cp` command can make a new copy of an existing item.

For instance, we can copy `file3` to a new file called `file4`:

```
cp file3 file4
```

Unlike the `mv` operation, after which `file3` would no longer exist, we now have both `file3` and `file4`.

Note: As with the `mv` command, it is possible to overwrite a file if you are not careful about the filename you are using as the target of the operation. For instance, if file4 already existed in the above example, its contents would be completely replaced by the contents of `file3`.

In order to copy directories, you must include the `-r` option in the command. This stands for "recursive," as it copies the directory, plus all of the directory's contents. This option is necessary with directories, regardless of whether the directory is empty. For instance, to copy the `some` directory structure to a new structure called `again`, we could type:

```
cp -r some again
```

Unlike with files, with which an existing destination would lead to an overwrite, if the target is an *existing directory*, the file or directory is copied *into* the target:

```
cp file1 again
```

This will create a new copy of `file1` and place it inside of the `again` directory.

Removing Files and Directories with "rm" and "rmdir"

To delete a file, you can use the `rm` command.

Note: Be extremely careful when using any destructive command like `rm`. There is no "undo" command for these actions so it is possible to accidentally destroy important files permanently.

To remove a regular file, just pass it to the `rm` command:

```
cd
rm file4
```

Likewise, to remove *empty* directories, we can use the `rmdir` command. This will only succeed if there is nothing in the directory in question. For instance, to remove the `example` directory within the `testing` directory, we can type:

```
rmdir testing/example
```
If you wish to remove a *non-empty* directory, you will have to use the rm command again. This time, you will have to pass the -r option, which removes all of the directory's contents recursively, plus the directory itself.

For instance, to remove the again directory and everything within it, we can type:

```
rm -r again
```
Once again, it is worth reiterating that these are permanent actions. Be entirely sure that the command you typed is the one that you wish to execute.

Editing Files

Currently, we know how to manipulate files as objects, but we have not learned how to actually edit and add content to them. The nano command is one of the simplest command-line Linux text editors, and is a great starting point for beginners. It operates somewhat similarly to the less program we discussed earlier, in that it occupies the entire terminal for the duration of its use. The nano editor can open existing files, or create a file. If you want to create a new file, you can give it a name when you call the nano editor, or later on, when you wish to save your content.

We can open the `file1` file for editing by typing:

```
cd
nano file1
```

The `nano` application will open the file (which is currently blank). The interface looks something like this:

```
   GNU nano 2.2.6                        File: file1


                                        [    Read    0
lines ]
^G Get Help     ^O WriteOut     ^R Read File   ^Y
Prev Page    ^K Cut Text     ^C Cur Pos
^X Exit           ^J Justify      ^W Where Is    ^V
Next Page    ^U UnCut Text ^T To Spell
```

Along the top, we have the name of the application and the name of the file we are editing. In the middle, the content of the file, currently blank, is displayed. Along the bottom, we have a number of key combinations that indicate some basic controls for the editor. For each of these, the ^ character means the `CTRL` key.

To get help from within the editor, type:

```
CTRL-G
```

When you are finished browsing the help, type `CTRL-X` to get back to your document.

Type in or modify any text you would like. For this example, we will just type these two sentences:

```
Hello there.
```

```
Here is some text.
```

To save type:

```
CTRL-O
```

This is the letter "o," not a zero. It will ask you to confirm the name of the file you wish to save to:

```
File Name to Write: file1
^G Get Help          M-D DOS Format        M-A
Append               M-B Backup File
^C Cancel            M-M Mac Format        M-P
Prepend
```

As you can see, the options at the bottom have also changed. These are contextual, meaning they will change depending on what you are trying to do. If file1 is still the file you wish to write to, hit "ENTER."

If we make additional changes and wish to save the file and exit the program, we will see a similar prompt. Add a new line, and then try to exit the program by typing:

```
CTRL-X
```

If you have not saved after making your modification, you will be asked whether you wish to save the modifications you made:

```
Save   modified   buffer   (ANSWERING   "No"   WILL
DESTROY CHANGES) ?
 Y Yes
 N No                ^C Cancel
```

You can type "Y" to save your changes, "N" to discard your changes and exit, or "CTRL-C" to cancel the exit operation. If you choose to save, you will be given the same file prompt that you received before, confirming that you want to save the changes to the same file. Press ENTER to save the file and exit the editor.

You can see the contents of the file you created using either the cat command to display the contents, or the less command to open the file for viewing. After viewing with less, remember that you should hit q to get back to the terminal.

```
less file1
Hello there.

Here is some text.

Another line.
```

Chapter Ten: UNIX

SHELL SCRIPTING

Time is precious. It does not make sense to waste time typing a frequently used sequence of commands at a command prompt, more especially if they are abnormally long or complex. Scripting is a way by which one can alleviate this problem by automating these command sequences in order to make life at the shell easier and more productive. Scripting is all about making the computer, the tool, do the work. By the end of this tutorial you will have a good understanding of the kind of scripting languages available for Unix and how to apply them to your problems. UNIX contains many wonderful and strange commands that can be very useful in the world of scripting, the more tools you know and the better you know them, the more use you will find for them. Most of the Unix commands and many of the built-in commands have `man` pages; `man` pages contain the usage instructions pertaining to the parent tool. They are not always very clear and may require reading several times. In order to access a man page in Unix the following command sequence is applied:

```
man command
```

If a man page exists for the command specified the internal viewer will be invoked and you will be able to read about the various options and usage instructions.

Shell Scripting Introduction

UNIX uses shells to accept commands given by the user; there are quite a few different shells available. The most commonly used shells are SH (Bourne SHell) CSH (C SHell) and KSH (Korn SHell), most of the other shells you encounter will be variants of these shells and will share the same syntax, KSH is based on SH as is BASH (Bourne again shell). TCSH (Extended C SHell) is based on CSH.

The various shells all have built in functions which allow for the creation of shell scripts, that is, the stringing together of shell commands and constructs to automate repetitive tasks in order to make life easier for the user.

With all these different shells available, what shell should we use? This is debatable. For the purpose of this tutorial we will be using SH because it is practically guaranteed to be available on most Unix systems and be supported by the SH based shells. Your default shell may not be SH. Fortunately we do not have to be using a specific shell in order to exploit its features because we can specify the shell we want to interpret our shell script within the script itself by including the following in the first line.

```
#!/path/to/shell
```

Usually anything following (#) is interpreted as a comment and ignored but if it occurs on the first line with a (!) following it is treated as being special and the filename following the (!) is considered to point to the location of the shell that should interpret the script.

When a script is "executed", it is being interpreted by an invocation of the shell that is running it. Hence, the shell is said to be running non-interactively, when the shell is used "normally" it is said to be running interactively.

Note: There are many variations of the basic commands and extra information which is too specific to be mentioned in this short tutorial, you should read the man page for your shell to get a more comprehensive idea of the options available to you. This tutorial will concentrate on highlighting the most often used and useful commands and constructs.

Command Redirection and Pipelines

By default a normal command accepts input from standard input, which we abbreviate to stdin, standard input is the command line in the form of arguments passed to the command. By default a normal command directs its output to standard output, which we abbreviate to stdout, standard output is usually the console display. For some commands this may be the desired action but other times we may wish to get our input for a command from somewhere other than stdin and direct our output to somewhere other than stdout. This is done by redirection:

We use > to redirect stdout to a file, for instance, if we wanted to redirect a directory listing generated by the **ls** we could do the following:

```
ls > file
```

We use < to specify that we want the command immediately before the redirection symbol to get its input from the source specified immediately after the symbol, for instance, we could redirect the input to `grep` (which searches for strings within files) so that it comes from a file like this:

```
grep searchterm < file
```

We use >> to append stdout to a file, for example, if we wanted to append the date to the end of a file we would redirect the output from `date` like so:

```
date >> file
```

One can redirect standard error (stderr) to a file by using **2>**, if we wanted to redirect the standard error from commandA to a file we would use:

```
commmandA 2>
```

Pipes are another form of redirection that are used to chain commands so that powerful composite commands can be constructed, the pipe symbol '|' takes the stdout from the command preceding it and redirects it to the command following it:

```
ls -l | grep searchword | sort -r
```

The example above firsts requests a long (-l directory listing of the current directory using the `ls` command, the output from this is then piped to `grep` which filters out all the listings containing the searchword and then finally pipes this through to `sort` which then sorts the output in reverse (-r, `sort` then passes the output on normally to stdout.

Variables

When a script starts, all environment variables are turned into shell variables. New variables can be instantiated like this:

```
name=value
```

You must do it exactly like that, with no spaces, the name must only be made up of alphabetic characters, numeric characters and underscores; it cannot begin with a numeric character. You should avoid using keywords like *for* or anything like that, the interpreter will let you use them but doing so can lead to obfuscated code ;)

Variables are referenced like this: $*name*, here is an example:

```
#!/bin/sh
msg1=Hello
msg2=There!
echo $msg1 $msg2
```

This would echo "Hello There!" to the console display, if you want to assign a string to a variable and the string contains spaces you should enclose the string in double quotes ("), the double quotes tell the shell to take the contents literally and ignore keywords, however, a few keywords are still processed. You can still use $ within a (") quoted string to include variables:

```
#!/bin/sh
msg1="one"
msg2="$msg1 two"
msg3="$msg2 three"
echo $msg3
```

Would echo "one two three" to the screen. The escape character can also be used within a double quoted section to output special characters, the escape character is "\", it outputs the character immediately following it literally so \\ would output \. A special case is when the escape character is followed by a newline; the shell ignores the newline character, which allows the spreading of long commands that must be executed on a single line in reality over multiple lines within the script. The escape character can be used anywhere, except within single quotes.

Surrounding anything with single quotes causes it to be treated as literal text that will be passed on exactly as intended, this can be useful for sending command sequences to other files in order to create new scripts because the text between the single quotes will remain untouched. For example:

```
#!/bin/sh
echo 'msg="Hello World!"' > hello
echo 'echo $msg' >> hello
chmod 700 hello
./hello
```

This would cause "msg="Hello World!" to be echoed and redirected to the file hello, "echo $msg" would then be echoed and redirected to the file hello but this time appended to the end. The *chmod* line changes the file permissions of hello so that we can execute it. The final line executes **hello** causing it output "Hello World." If we had not used literal quotes we would not have had to use escape characters to ensure that ($)

and (") were echoed to the file, this makes the code a little clearer.

A variable may be referenced like so ${VARIABLENAME}, this allows one to place characters immediately preceding the variable like ${VARIABLENAME}aaa without the shell interpreting aaa as being part of the variable name.

Command Line Arguments

Command line arguments are treated as special variables within the script, the reason I am calling them variables is because they can be changed with the **shift** command. The command line arguments are enumerated in the following manner $0, $1, $2, $3, $4, $5, $6, $7, $8 and $9. $0 is special in that it corresponds to the name of the script itself. $1 is the first argument, $2 is the second argument and so on. To reference after the ninth argument you must enclose the number in brackets like this ${nn}. You can use the **shift** command to shift the arguments 1 variable to the left so that $2 becomes $1, $1 becomes$0 and so on, $0 gets scrapped because it has nowhere to go, this can be useful to process all the arguments using a loop, using one variable to reference the first argument and **shifting** until you have exhausted the arguments list.

As well as the command line arguments there are some special built-in variables:

- $# represents the parameter count. Useful for controlling loop constructs that need to process each parameter.
- $@ expands to all the parameters separated by spaces. Useful for passing all the parameters to some other function or program.
- $- expands to the flags(options) the shell was invoked with. Useful for controlling program flow based on the flags set.
- $$ expands to the process id of the shell innovated to run the script. Useful for creating unique temporary filenames relative to this instantiation of the script.

Note: The command line arguments will be referred to as parameters from now on, this is because SH also allows the definition of functions which can take parameters and when called the $nfamily will be redefined, hence these variables are always parameters, its just that in the case of the parent script the parameters are passed via the command line. One exception is $0which is always set to the name of the parent script regardless of whether it is inside a function or not.

Command Substitution

In the words of the SH manual *"Command substitution allows the output of a command to be substituted in place of the command name itself"*. There are two ways this can be done. The first is to enclose the command like this:

```
$(command)
```

The second is to enclose the command in back quotes like this:

```
`command`
```

The command will be executed in a sub-shell environment and the standard output of the shell will replace the command substitution when the command finishes.

Arithmetic Expansion

Arithmetic expansion is also allowed and comes in the form:

```
$((expression))
```

The value of the expression will replace the substitution. Eg:

```
!#/bin/sh
echo $((1 + 3 + 4))
```

Will echo "8" to stdout

Control Constructs

The flow of control within SH scripts is done via four main constructs; if...   then...   elif...,   else..., do..., while..., for... and case....

If.. Then.. Elif.. Else

This construct takes the following generic form; the parts enclosed within ([) and (]) are optional:

```
if list
then list
[elif list
then list] ...
[else list]
fi
```

When a Unix command exits it exits with what is known as an *exit status*, this indicates to anyone who wants to know the degree of success a command, usually when a command executes without error it terminates with an exit status of zero. An exit status of some other value would indicates that an error has occurred, the details of which are specific to the command. The commands' man pages detail the exit status messages.

A list is defined in the SH as "*a sequence of zero or more commands separated by newlines, semicolons, or ampersands, and optionally terminated by one of these three characters.*" Hence in the generic definition of the *if* above the list will determine which of the execution paths the script takes. For example, there is a command called `test` on UNIX, which evaluates an expression and if it evaluates true will return zero and will return one otherwise, this is how we can test conditions in the *list* part(s) of the *if* construct because `test` is a command.

We do not actually have to type the `test` command directly into the *list* to use it; it can be implied by encasing the test case within ([) and (]) characters, as illustrated by the following (silly) example:

```
#!/bin/sh
if [ "$1" = "1" ]
then
    echo "The first choice is nice"
elif [ "$1" = "2" ]
then
    echo "The second choice is just as nice"
elif [ "$1" = "3" ]
then
    echo "The third choice is excellent"
else
    echo "I see you were wise enough not to
choose"
    echo "You win"
fi
```

What this example does is compare the first parameter (command line argument in this case) with the strings "1", "2" and "3" using **test**s' (=) test which compares two strings for equality, if any of them match it prints out the corresponding message. If none of them match it prints out the final case. OK the example is silly and actually flawed (the user still wins even if they type in (4) or something) but it illustrates how the *if* statement works.

Notice that there are spaces between (if) and ([), ([) and the test and the test and (]), these spaces must be present otherwise the shell will complain. There must also be spaces between the operator and operands of the test otherwise it will not work properly. Notice how it starts with (if) and ends with (fi), also, notice how (then) is on a separate line to the test above it and that (else) does not require a (then) statement. You must construct this construct exactly like this for it to work properly.

It is also possible to integrate logical AND and OR into the testing, by using two tests separated by either "&&" or "||" respectively. For example, we could replace the third test case in the example above with:

```
elif [ "$1" = "3"] || [ "$1" = "4" ]
then echo "The third choi...
```

The script would print out "The third choice is excellent" if the first parameter was either "3" OR "4". To illustrate the use of "&&" we could replace the third test case with:

```
elif [ "$1" = "3"] || [ "$2" = "4" ]
```

```
then echo "The third choi...
```

The script would print out "The third choice is excellent" if and only if the first parameter was "3" AND the second parameter was "4".

"&&" and "||" are both lazily evaluating which means that in the case of "&&", if the first test fails it won't bother evaluating the second because the list will only be true if they *BOTH* pass and since one has already failed there is no point wasting time evaluating the second. In the case of "||" if the first test passes it won't bother evaluating the second test because we only need *ONE* of the tests to pass for the whole list to pass. See the test man page for the list of tests possible (other than the string equality test mentioned here).

Do...While

The *Do...While* takes the following generic form:

```
while list
do list
done
```

In the words of the SH manual *"The two lists are executed repeatedly while the exit status of the first list is zero."* There is a variation on this that uses until in place of while which executes *until* the exit status of the first list is zero. Here is an example use of the `while` statement:

```
#!/bin/sh
count=$1                                              #
Initialise count to first parameter
while [ $count -gt 0 ]                                #
while count is greater than 10 do
do
    echo $count seconds till supper time!
    count=$(expr $count -1)                           #
decrement count by 1
    sleep 1                                           #
sleep for a second using the Unix sleep command
done
echo Supper time!!, YEAH!!                            # were
finished
```

If called from the command line with an argument of 4 this script will output

```
4 seconds till supper time!
3 seconds till supper time!
2 seconds till supper time!
1 seconds till supper time!
Supper time!!, YEAH!!
```

You can see that this time we have used the `-gt` of the `test` command implicitly called by '[' and ']', which stands for greater than. Pay careful attention to the formatting and spacing.

For

The syntax of the `for` command is:

```
for variable in word ...
do list
done
```

The SH manual states *"The words are expanded, and then the list is executed repeatedly with the variable set to each word in turn."* A word is essentially some other variable that contains a list of values of some sort, the *for* construct assigns each of the values in the word to variable and then variable can be used within the body of the construct, upon completion of the body variable will be assigned the next value in word until there are no more values in word. This example should make this clearer:

```
#!/bin/sh
fruitlist="Apple Pear Tomato Peach Grape"
for fruit in $fruitlist
do
    if [ "$fruit" = "Tomato" ] || [ "$fruit" =
"Peach" ]
    then
        echo "I like ${fruit}es"
    else
        echo "I like ${fruit}s"
    fi
done
```

In this example, *fruitlist* is word, *fruit* is variable and the body of the statement outputs how much this person loves various fruits but includes an *if... then... else* statement to deal with the correct addition of letters to describe the plural version of the fruit, notice that the variable *fruit* was expressed like *${fruit}* because otherwise the shell would have interpreted the preceding letter(s) as being part of the variable and echoed nothing because we have not defined the variables *fruits* and *fruites* When executed this script will output:

```
I like Apples
I like Pears
I like Tomatoes
I like Peachs
I like Grapes
```

Within the *for* construct, do and done may be replaced by '{' and '}'.

Case

The `case` construct has the following syntax:

```
case word in
pattern) list ;;
...

esac
```

An example of this should make things clearer:

```
!#/bin/sh
case $1
in
1) echo 'First Choice';;
2) echo 'Second Choice';;
*) echo 'Other Choice';;
esac
```

"1", "2" and "*" are patterns, word is compared to each pattern and if a match is found the body of the corresponding pattern is executed, we have used "*" to represent everything, since this is checked last we will still catch "1" and "2" because they are checked first. In our example word is "$1", the first parameter, hence if the script is ran with the argument "1" it will output "First Choice", "2" "Second Choice" and anything else "Other Choice". In this example we compared against numbers (essentially still a string comparison however) but the pattern can be more complex, see the SH man page for more information.

Functions

The syntax of an SH function is defined as follows:

```
name ( ) command
```

It is usually laid out like this:

```
name() {
commands
}
```

A function will return with a default exit status of zero, one can return different exit statuses by using the notation return *exit status*. Variables can be defined locally within a function using local *name=value*. The example below shows the use of a user defined increment function:

Increment Function Example

```
#!/bin/sh
inc() { ❶                               # The increment is
defined first so we can use it
    echo $(($1 + $2))                   # We echo the result
of the first parameter plus the second parameter
}

                                        # We check to see
that all the command line arguments are present
if [ "$1" "" ] || [ "$2" = "" ] || [ "$3" = "" ]
then
    echo USAGE:
    echo "   counter startvalue incrementvalue endvalue"
else
    count=$1                            # Rename are
variables with clearer names
    value=$2
    end=$3
    while [ $count -lt $end ]           # Loop while count is
less than end
    do
        echo $count
        count=$(inc $count $value)    ❷# Call increment
with count and value as parameters
    done                                # so that count is
incremented by value
fi
```

```
inc() {
    echo $(($1 + $2))
}
```

The function is defined and opened with inc() {, the line echo $(($1 + $2)) uses the notation for arithmetic expression substitution which is $((*expression*)) to enclose the expression, $1 + $2 which adds the first and second parameters passed to the function together, the echo bit at the start echoes them to standard output, we can catch this value by assigning the function call to a variable, as is illustrated by the function call.

```
count=$(inc $count $value)
```

We use command substitution which substitutes the value of a command to substitute the value of the function call whereupon it is assigned to the *count* variable. The command within the command substitution block is inc $count $value, the last two values being its parameters. Which are then referenced from within the function using $1 and $2. We could have used the other command substitution notation to call the function if we had wanted:

```
count=`inc $count $value`
```

Here is another example illustrating the scope of variables:

Variable Scope, Example

```
#!/bin/sh
inc() {
    local value=4
    echo "value is $value within the function\\n"
    echo "\\b\$1 is $1 within the function"
}

value=5
echo value is $value before the function
echo "\$1 is $1 before the function"
echo
```

```
echo -e $(inc $value)
echo
echo value is $value after the function
echo "\$1 is $1 after the function"
```

```
inc() {
    local value=4
    echo "value is $value within the function\\n"
    echo "\\b\$1 is $1 within the function"
}
```

We assign a local value to the variable *value* of 4. The next
three lines construct the output, remember that this is being
echoed to a buffer and will be replace the function call with all
that was passed to stdout within the function when the
function exits. So, the calling code will be replaced with
whatever we direct to standard output within the function. The
function is called like this:

```
echo -e $(inc $value)
```

We have passed the option -e to the **echo** command which
causes it to process C-style backslash escape characters, so we
can process any backslash escape characters which the string
generated by the function call contains. If we just echo the
lines we want to be returned by the function it will not pass the
newline character onto the buffer even if we explicitly include
it with an escape character reference so what we do is actually

include the sequence of characters that will produce a new line within the string so that when it is echoed by the calling code with the -e the escape characters will be processed and the newlines will be placed where we want them.

```
echo "value is $value within the function\\n"
```

Notice how the newline has been inserted with \\n, the first two backslashes indicate that we want to echo a backslash because within double quotes a backslash indicates to process the next character literally, we have to do this because we are only between double quotes and not the literal-text single quotes. If we had used single quotes we would had have to echo the bit with the newline in separately from the bit that contains $value otherwise $value would not be expanded.

```
echo "\\b\$1 is $1 within the function"
```

This is our second line, and is contained within double quotes so that the variable $1 will be expanded, \\b is included so that \b will be placed in the echoed line and our calling code processes this as a backspace character. If we do not do that the shell prefixes a space to the second line, the backspace removes this space.

The output from this script called with 2 as the first argument is:

```
value is 5 before the function
$1 is 2 before the function

value is 4 within the function
$1 is 5 within the function

value is 5 after the function
$1 is 2 after the function
```

Tip: You can use ". DIRECTORY/common.sh" to import functions from a script called common.sh in DIRECTORY, a quick example is shown below, first is test.sh:

```
#!/bin/sh
. ./common.sh
if [ "$1" = "" ]; then
    echo USAGE:
    echo "sh test.sh type"
    exit
fi

if `validtype $1`; then
    echo Valid type
else
    echo Invalid type
fi
```

Here is common.sh:

```
#!/bin/sh
validtype() {
    if [ "$1" = "TYPEA" ] ||
       [ "$1" = "TYPEB" ] ||
       [ "$1" = "TYPEC" ] ||
       [ "$1" = "TYPED" ] ||
       [ "$1" = "TYPEE" ];
    then
        exit 0
    else
        exit 1
    fi
}
```

Chapter Eleven:

SHELL BASIC OPERATOR

Each shell supports various operators. This chapter is based on default shell (Bourne) so we are going to cover all the important Bourne Shell operators in this tutorial.

We will discuss the following operators –

- – Arithmetic Operators.
- – Relational Operators.
- – Boolean Operators.
- – String Operators.
- – File Test Operators.

The Bourne shell did not originally have any mechanism to perform simple arithmetic but it uses external programs, either `awk` or the must simpler program `expr`.

Here is simple example to add two numbers –

```
#!/bin/sh

val=`expr 2 + 2`
echo "Total value : $val"
```

This produces the following result –

```
Total value : 4
```

Note:

- There must be spaces between operators and expressions for example 2+2 is not correct, it should be written as 2 + 2.

- Complete expressions should be enclosed between `` ` ` ``, inverted commas.

Arithmetic Operators

The following are arithmetic operators supported by the Bourne Shell.

Assume variable 'a' holds 10 and variable 'b' holds 20 then –

Example, using all the arithmetic operators –

```
#!/bin/sh

a=10
b=20
val=`expr $a + $b`
echo "a + b : $val"

val=`expr $a - $b`
echo "a - b : $val"
```

```
val=`expr $a \* $b`
echo "a * b : $val"


val=`expr $b / $a`
echo "b / a : $val"


val=`expr $b % $a`
echo "b % a : $val"


if [ $a == $b ]
then
    echo "a is equal to b"
fi


if [ $a != $b ]
then
    echo "a is not equal to b"
fi
```

This produces the following result –

```
a + b : 30
a - b : -10
a * b : 200
b / a : 2
b % a : 0
a is not equal to b
```

Note:

- There must be spaces between operators and expressions for example 2+2 is not correct, whereas it should be written as 2 + 2.

- Complete expression should be enclosed between `` ``, inverted commas.

- You should use \ on the * symbol for multiplication.

- **The if...then...fi** statement is a decision-making statement, which will be explained in the next chapter.

Operator	Description	Example
+	Addition - Adds values on either side of the operator	`expr $a + $b` will give 30
-	Subtraction - Subtracts right hand operand from left hand operand	`expr $a - $b` will give -10
*	Multiplication - Multiplies values on either side of the operator	`expr $a \* $b` will give 200
/	Division - Divides left hand operand by right hand operand	`expr $b / $a` will give 2
%	Modulus - Divides left hand operand by right hand operand and returns remainder	`expr $b % $a` will give 0

=	Assignment - Assign right operand in left operand	a=$b would assign value of b into a
==	Equality - Compares two numbers, if both are same then returns true.	[$a == $b] would return false.
!=	Not Equality - Compares two numbers, if both are different then returns true.	[$a != $b] would return true.

It is very important to note that all the conditional expressions should be put inside square braces with one spaces around them, for example [$a == $b] is correct whereas [$a==$b] is incorrect.

All the arithmetical calculations are done using long integers.

Relational Operators:

Bourne Shell supports the following relational operators, which are specific to numeric values. These operators will not work for string values unless their value is numeric. For example, the following operators check a relation between 10 and 20 as well as in between "10" and "20" but not in between "ten" and "twenty". Assume variable a holds 10 and variable b holds 20 then –

This example uses all the relational operators –

```
#!/bin/sh
```

```
a=10
b=20

if [ $a -eq $b ]
then
   echo "$a -eq $b : a is equal to b"
else
   echo "$a -eq $b: a is not equal to b"
fi

if [ $a -ne $b ]
then
   echo "$a -ne $b: a is not equal to b"
else
   echo "$a -ne $b : a is equal to b"
fi

if [ $a -gt $b ]
then
   echo "$a -gt $b: a is greater than b"
else
   echo "$a -gt $b: a is not greater than b"
fi

if [ $a -lt $b ]
then
   echo "$a -lt $b: a is less than b"
```

```
else
    echo "$a -lt $b: a is not less than b"
fi


if [ $a -ge $b ]
then
    echo "$a -ge $b: a is greater or  equal to b"
else
    echo "$a -ge $b: a is not greater or equal to b"
fi


if [ $a -le $b ]
then
    echo "$a -le $b: a is less or  equal to b"
else
    echo "$a -le $b: a is not less or equal to b"
fi
```

This produces the following result –

```
10 -eq 20: a is not equal to b

10 -ne 20: a is not equal to b

10 -gt 20: a is not greater than b

10 -lt 20: a is less than b

10 -ge 20: a is not greater or equal to b

10 -le 20: a is less or  equal to b
```

Note:

- There must be spaces between operators and expressions for example 2+2 is not correct, whereas it should be written as 2 + 2.

- **if...then...else...fi** statement is a decision making statement which will be explained in the next chapter.

Operator	Description	E.
-eq	Checks if the value of two operands are equal, if yes then condition becomes true.	[ ] tr
-ne	Checks if the value of two operands are equal, if values are not equal then condition becomes true.	[ ]
-gt	Checks if the value of left operand is greater than the value of right operand, if yes then condition becomes true.	[ ] tr
-lt	Checks if the value of left operand is less than the value of right operand, if yes then condition becomes true.	[ ] is
-ge	Checks if the value of left operand is greater than or equal to the value of right operand, if yes then condition becomes true.	[ ] tr
-le	Checks if the value of left operand is less than or equal to the value of right operand, if yes then condition becomes true.	[ ]

It is very important to note that all the conditional expressions should be put inside square braces with one spaces around them, for example [$a <= $b] is correct whereas [$a <= $b] is incorrect.

Boolean Operators

The Bourne Shell supports the following boolean operators.

Assume variable 'a' holds 10 and variable 'b' holds 20 then –

This example uses all the boolean operators –

```
#!/bin/sh

a=10
b=20

if [ $a != $b ]
then
    echo "$a != $b : a is not equal to b"
else
    echo "$a != $b: a is equal to b"
fi

if [ $a -lt 100 -a $b -gt 15 ]
then
    echo "$a -lt 100 -a $b -gt 15 : returns true"
else
```

```
    echo "$a -lt 100 -a $b -gt 15 : returns false"
fi


if [ $a -lt 100 -o $b -gt 100 ]

then

    echo "$a -lt 100 -o $b -gt 100 : returns true"

else

    echo "$a -lt 100 -o $b -gt 100 : returns false"
fi


if [ $a -lt 5 -o $b -gt 100 ]

then

    echo "$a -lt 100 -o $b -gt 100 : returns true"

else

    echo "$a -lt 100 -o $b -gt 100 : returns false"
fi
```

This produces the following result –

```
10 != 20 : a is not equal to b

10 -lt 100 -a 20 -gt 15 : returns true

10 -lt 100 -o 20 -gt 100 : returns true

10 -lt 5 -o 20 -gt 100 : returns false
```

Note:

- There must be spaces between operators and expressions for example 2+2 is not correct, whereas it should be written as 2 + 2.

Operator	Description	Example
!	This is a logical negation. This inverts a true condition into false and vice versa.	[! false] is true.
-o	This is a logical OR. If one of the operands were true then condition would be true.	[$a -lt 20 -o $b -gt 100] is true.
-a	This is a logical AND. If both the operands were true then condition would be true otherwise, it would be false.	[$a -lt 20 -a $b -gt 100] is false.

String Operators

The Bourne Shell supports the following string operators.

Assume variable 'a' holds "abc" and variable 'b' holds "efg" then −

This example uses all the string operators −

```
#!/bin/sh

a="abc"
b="efg"

if [ $a = $b ]
then
    echo "$a = $b : a is equal to b"
else
```

```
    echo "$a = $b: a is not equal to b"
fi


if [ $a != $b ]
then
    echo "$a != $b : a is not equal to b"
else
    echo "$a != $b: a is equal to b"
fi


if [ -z $a ]
then
    echo "-z $a : string length is zero"
else
    echo "-z $a : string length is not zero"
fi


if [ -n $a ]
then
    echo "-n $a : string length is not zero"
else
    echo "-n $a : string length is zero"
fi


if [ $a ]
then
    echo "$a : string is not empty"
```

```
else
   echo "$a : string is empty"
fi
```

This produces the following result –

```
abc = efg: a is not equal to b
abc != efg : a is not equal to b
-z abc : string length is not zero
-n abc : string length is not zero
abc : string is not empty
```

Note:

- There must be spaces between operators and expressions for example 2+2 is not correct, whereas it should be written as 2 + 2.

Operator	Description	Example
=	Checks if the value of two operands is equal, if yes then condition becomes true.	[$a = $b] is not true.
!=	Checks if the value of two operands are equal, if values are not equal then condition becomes true.	[$a != $b] is true.
-z	Checks if the given string operand size is zero. If it is zero length then it returns true.	[-z $a] is not true.

| -n | Checks if the given string operand size is non-zero. If it is non-zero length then it returns true. | [-z $a] is not false. |
| **str** | Check if str is not the empty string. If it is empty then it returns false. | [$a] is not false. |

File Test Operators

The following operators test various properties associated with a Unix file.

Assume a variable `file` holds an existing file name "test" whose size is 100 bytes and has read, write and execute permissions –

This example uses all the file test operators –

```
#!/bin/sh

file="/var/www/tutorialspoint/unix/test.sh"

if [ -r $file ]
then
   echo "File has read access"
else
   echo "File does not have read access"
fi


if [ -w $file ]
```

```
then

    echo "File has write permission"

else

    echo "File does not have write permission"

fi


if [ -x $file ]

then

    echo "File has execute permission"

else

    echo "File does not have execute permission"

fi


if [ -f $file ]

then

    echo "File is an ordinary file"

else

    echo "This is special file"

fi


if [ -d $file ]

then

    echo "File is a directory"

else

    echo "This is not a directory"

fi
```

```
if [ -s $file ]

then

    echo "File size is zero"

else

    echo "File size is not zero"

fi


if [ -e $file ]

then

    echo "File exists"

else

    echo "File does not exist"

fi
```

This produces the following result –

```
File has read access

File has write permission

File has execute permission

File is an ordinary file

This is not a directory

File size is zero

File exists
```

Note:

- There must be spaces between operators and expressions for example 2+2 is not correct, whereas it should be written as 2 + 2.

Operator	Description	Example
-b file	Checks if file is a block special file if yes then condition becomes true.	[-b $file] is false.
-c file	Checks if file is a character special file if yes then condition becomes true.	[-c $file] is false.
-d file	Check if file is a directory if yes then condition becomes true.	[-d $file] is not true.
-f file	Check if file is an ordinary file as opposed to a directory or special file if yes then condition becomes true.	[-f $file] is true.
-g file	Checks if file has its set group ID (SGID) bit set if yes then condition becomes true.	[-g $file] is false.
-k file	Checks if file has its sticky bit set if yes then condition becomes true.	[-k $file] is false.
-p file	Checks if file is a named pipe if yes then condition becomes true.	[-p $file] is false.
-t file	Checks if file descriptor is open and associated with a terminal if yes then condition becomes true.	[-t $file] is false.
-u file	Checks if file has its set user id (SUID) bit set if yes then condition becomes true.	[-u $file] is false.
-r file	Checks if file is readable if yes then condition becomes true.	[-r $file] is true.

-w file	Checks if file is writable if yes then condition becomes true.	[-w $file] is true.
-x file	Checks if file is execute if yes then condition becomes true.	[-x $file] is true.
-s file	Checks if file has size greater than 0 if yes then condition becomes true.	[-s $file] is true.
-e file	Checks if file exists. Is true even if file is a directory but exists.	[-e $file] is true.

Run The .Sh File Shell Script In Linux / Unix

After downloading the software, the .sh file is nothing but the shell script to install a given application or to perform other tasks under UNIX like operating systems. The easiest way to run .sh shell script in Linux or UNIX is to type either of the following commands. Open the terminal (your shell prompt) and type the command:

```
sh file.sh
```
OR

```
bash file.sh
```

.sh As Root User

Sometimes you will need to install an application that requires root level privileges. Root access is disabled by default on many Linux and UNIX like systems. Simply use sudo or su as follows:

```
sudo bash filename.sh
```
Type your password. Another option is to use the su command as follows to become superuser:

```
su -
```
Type root user password and finally run your script:

```
bash filename.sh
```

chmod Command: Run Shell Script In Linux

Another recommended option is to set an executable permission using the chmod command as follows:

```
chmod +x file.sh
```
Now you can run the .sh file.

```
./file.sh
```

Chapter Twelve:

SHELL EMBEDDING AND OPTIONS

This chapter investigates tyke shells, implanted shells and shell alternatives.

Shell installing

Shells can be installed to work on a command line; the command line can bring forth new procedures containing a fork of the present shell. You can use variables to demonstrate that the new shells are made. The variable $var1 just exists in the (interim) sub shell.

```
[paul@RHELv4u3 gen]$ reverberation $var1

[paul@RHELv4u3  gen]$  reverberation  $(var1=5;echo
$var1)

5

[paul@RHELv4u3 gen]$ reverberation $var1

[paul@RHELv4u3 gen]$
```

You can install a shell into an inserted shell; this is called settled implanting of shells.

```
paul@deb503:~$ A=shell
```

```
paul@deb503:~$ reverberation $C$B$A $(B=sub;echo
$C$B$A; reverberation $(C=sub;echo $C$B$A))
```

shell subshell subsubshell

Backticks

Single installation can change your present index and uses
backticks instead of dollar section to implant.

```
[paul@RHELv4u3 ~]$ reverberation `cd/and so forth; ls -
d * | grep pass`

passwd-passwd.OLD

[paul@RHELv4u3 ~]$
```

The backticks /() and the $() documentation can be used to
implant a shell.

Backticks or single quotes

Putting the installing between backticks utilizes one character
not exactly the dollar and bracket combo. Be cautious on the
other hand, backticks are frequently mistaken for single
quotes.

The specialized contrast in the middle of " and ` is critical!

```
[paul@RHELv4u3 gen]$ reverberation `var1=5;echo $var1`

[paul@RHELv4u3 gen]$ reverberation 'var1=5;echo $var1'

var1=5;echo $var1

[paul@RHELv4u3 gen]$
```

Shell Alternatives

Both `set` and `unset` are built-in shell commands, which are used to set alternatives to the bash shell. The following case will clear up this. The shell will treat unset variables as an unimportant variable. By setting the – u alternative, the shell will treat any reference to unset variables as an error.

```
[paul@RHEL4b ~]$ reverberation $var123

[paul@RHEL4b ~]$ set - u

[paul@RHEL4b ~]$ reverberation $var123

- bash: var123: unbound variable

[paul@RHEL4b ~]$ set +u

[paul@RHEL4b ~]$ reverberation $var123

[paul@RHEL4b ~]$
```

To rundown all the set choices for your shell, use reverberation $-. The noclobber (or - C).

```
[paul@RHEL4b ~]$ reverberation $-

himBH

[paul@RHEL4b ~]$ set - C ; set - u

[paul@RHEL4b ~]$ reverberation $-

himuBCH

[paul@RHEL4b ~]$ set +C ; set +u
```

```
[paul@RHEL4b ~]$ reverberation $-

himBH

[paul@RHEL4b ~]$
```

When writing a set without alternatives, you get a rundown of all variables without capacity, when the shell is in posix mode, you can set bash in posix mode writing set - o posix.

Practice: Shell Installing

1. Discover the rundown of shell choices in the man page of bash. What is the contrast between situated - u and set - o nounset?

2. Actuate nounset in your shell. Test if it demonstrates an error message when using non-existing variables.

3. Deactivate nounset.

4. Execute `disc/var` and `ls` in an installed shell.
   The reverberation command is expected to demonstrate the after effects of the `ls` command. Precluding will cause the shell to execute the first document as a command.

5. Add the variable `embvar` into an inserted shell and reverberation it. Does the variable exist in your present shell now?

6. Clarify what "`set - x`" does. Can this be useful? (Optional)

7. Given the accompanying screenshot, add four characters to the command so that the aggregate yield is FirstMiddleLast. [paul@RHEL4b ~]$ reverberate First; resound Middle; reverberate Last.

8. Display a long listing (`ls - l`) of the passwd command utilizing the `which` command inside an installed shell.

15.4. Arrangement: shell inserting

1. Discover the rundown of shell alternatives in the man page of bash. What is the distinction between situated u and set - o nounset?

   Check the man of bash and look for nounset - both mean the same thing.

2. Add nounset to your shell. Test that it demonstrates a lapse message when utilizing nonexisting variables.

   ```
   set - u
   ```

   Or

   ```
   set - o nounset
   ```

   Both lines have the same impact.

3. Deactivate nounset.

   ```
   set +u
   ```

   Or

   ```
   set +o nounset
   ```

4. Execute `album/var` and `ls` in an implanted shell.
   reverberation $(cd/var ; ls)

   The reverberation command is used to demonstrate the consequence of the ls command. Precluding will make the shell to execute the first document as a command.

5. Make the variable `embvar` in an implanted shell and reverberation it. Does the variable exist in your present shell?

   reverberation $(embvar=emb;echo $embvar) ; reverberation $embvar #the last resound fizzles

   $embvar does not exist in your present shell

6. Clarify what "`set - x`" does. Is this useful?

   It shows shell development for investigating your command.

(Optional)

7. Given the accompanying screenshot, add four characters to the command line so that the aggregate yield is FirstMiddleLast.

   [paul@RHEL4b ~]$ reverberate First; resound Middle; reverberate Last

   reverberation - n First; resound - n Middle; resound Last

8. Show a long posting (`ls - l`) of the passwd command using the "`which` command" inside an implanted shell.

   ls - l $(which passwd

Almost all-modern shell allows you to search command history if enabled by the user. History command can display the history list with line numbers, listed with a * have been modified by user.

Chapter Thirteen: SHELL

HISTORY SEARCH COMMAND

Type history at a shell prompt:

$ history

Output:

```
  6  du -c
  7  du -ch
  8  ls [01-15]*-2008
  9  ls -ld [01-15]*-2008
 10  ls -ld [1-15]*-2008
 11  ls -ld [0]*-2008
 12  ls -ld [01]*-2008
 13  rm -vrf [01]*-2008
 14  du -ch
 15  ls
 16  cd
 17  umount /mnt
 18  df -H
 19  vnstat
 20  yum update
 21  vnstat -m
 22  vnstat -m -i eth0
....
...
 996  ping router.nixcraft.in
 997  ssh vivek@p1.vpn.nixcraft.in
 998  alias
 999  ~/scripts/clean.rss --fetch
1000  vnstat
1001  ~/scripts/clean.rss  --update
```

To search for a particular command, enter:

```
$ history | grep command-name
$ history | egrep -i 'scp|ssh|ftp'
```

Emacs Line-Edit Mode Command History Searching

To find the command containing string, hit [CTRL]+[r] followed by search string:

```
(reverse-i-search):
```

To show the previous command, hit [CTRL] + [p]. You can also use up arrow key.

```
CTRL-p
```

To show the next command, hit [CTRL] +[n]. You can also use down arrow key.

```
CTRL-n
```

fc command

fc stands for either the `find` command or the `fix` command. For example to list the last 10 commands, enter:

```
$ fc -l 10
```

to list commands 130 through 150, enter:

```
$ fc -l 130 150
```

to list all commands since the last command beginning with

ssh, enter:

```
$ fc -l ssh
```

You can **edit commands** 1 through 5 using vi text editor, enter:

```
$ fc -e vi 1 5
```

Delete command history

The -c option causes the history list to be cleared by deleting all of the entries:

```
$ history -c
```

FILE NAME GLOBBING WITH *, ?, [ ]

Sometimes you want to manipulate a group of files, e.g., delete all of them, without having to perform the command on each file separately. For example, suppose we want to delete all of the **.c** files in a directory. A **wildcard** is a pattern, which **matches** something else. Two commonly used *nix wildcards are * (star) and **?** (question mark).

- Star (*) means zero or more characters
- Question Mark (?) means exactly one character
- Brackets ([]) represent a set of characters

Commands involving filenames specified with wildcards are expanded by the shell (this is called **globbing** after the name of a former program called **glob** which used to do this outside the shell).

The '*'

' **file*'** will match any filename which starts with the characters "file", and then is followed by zero or more occurrences of any character.

Examples

Suppose **Fred's** home directory contains the files,

- ☐ file01.cpp
- ☐ file02.cpp
- ☐ file03.cpp
- ☐ file1.cpp
- ☐ file01.o
- ☐ file02.o
- ☐ file03.o
- ☐ file1.o

To delete all of the **.c** files, type,

```
$ rm *.c
```

To delete file01.cpp and file01.o,

```
$ rm file01.*
```

The '?'

'?' Represents a single character.

Examples

Consider again Fred's home directory from the previous example.

Delete file01.o, file02.o and file03.o, but not file1.o,

```
$ rm file??.o
```

Delete file01.o, but not file01.cpp,

```
$ rm file01.?
```

The '[ ]' Glob

A set of characters can be specified with brackets [ ]. `'[ab]'` means the **single** character can be 'a 'OR 'b'. Ranges can also be specified (ex: `'[1-57-9]'` represents 1-5 OR 7-9).

Examples

Delete file02.cpp and file03.cpp from Fred's directory,

```
$ rm file0[23].cpp
```

This will delete any files that start with f or F (remember linux is case sensitive),

```
$rm [fF]*
```

To delete all files that start with the string **"file"** followed by a single letter type,

```
$ rm file[a-zA-Z]
```

The a-z and A-Z in the last example means all the letters in the range lowercase a-z or uppercase A-Z.

There is much more to wildcard matching, but this is enough to get you started.

More Examples

Remove all files that are exactly 1 character,

```
$rm ?
```

Let's say you have a directory named '9-15-2007-Backup-Really-Long-Name-blah...' Rather than typing the whole name, you could just type a subset of the string and use it with the cd command.

```
$ cd 9-15-2007*
```

If you have multiple folders that start with 9-15-2007, your directory will be changed to the first one alphabetically.

You can use file name globbing on most commands that accept files as arguments.

Chapter fourteen: UNIX -
SHELL INPUT/OUTPUT REDIRECTIONS

Most Unix system commands take input from your keyboard and send the resulting output back to your monitor. A command normally reads its input from a place called standard input, which is your keyboard by default. Similarly, a command normally writes its output to standard output, which is your monitor by default.

Output Redirection

The output from a command normally intended for standard output can be easily diverted to a file. This is known as output redirection:

If the notation > `file` is appended to any command that normally writes its output to standard output, the output of that command will be written to file instead of your terminal – Check following `who` command which would redirect complete output of the command to a file called users.

```
$ who > users
```

Notice that no output appears at the terminal. This is because the output has been redirected from the default standard output device (the terminal) into the specified file. If you check the *users* file then it should have this content –

```
$ cat users
oko          tty01    Sep 12 07:30
ai           tty15    Sep 12 13:32
ruth         tty21    Sep 12 10:10
pat          tty24    Sep 12 13:07
steve        tty25    Sep 12 13:03
$
```

If a command has its output redirected to a file and the file already contains some data, that data will be lost. Consider this example –

```
$ echo line 1 > users
$ cat users
line 1
$
```

You can use >> operator to append the output in an existing file as follows –

```
$ echo line 2 >> users
$ cat users
line 1
line 2
$
```

Input Redirection

Just as the output of a command can be redirected to a file, so can the input of a command be redirected from a file. As the greater-than sign > is used for output redirection, the less-than sign < is used to redirect the input of a command. The commands that normally take their input from standard input can have their input redirected from a file in this manner. For example, to count the number of lines in the file *users* generated above, you can execute the following command –

```
$ wc -l users
2 users
$
```

Here it produces the output 2 line. You can count the number of lines in the file by redirecting the standard input of the wc command from the file *users* –

```
$ wc -l < users
2
$
```

Note that there is a difference in the output produced by the two forms of the wc command. In the first case, the name of the file users is listed with the line count; in the second case, it is not. In the first case, wc knows that it is reading its input from the file users. In the second case, it only knows that it is reading its input from standard input so it does not display file name.

Here Document

A *here document* is used to redirect input into an interactive shell script or program. We can run an interactive program within a shell script without user action by supplying the required input for the interactive program, or interactive shell script.

The general format for a here document is –

```
command << delimiter
document
delimiter
```

Here the shell interprets the << operator as an instruction to read input until it finds a line containing the specified delimiter. All the input lines up to the line containing the delimiter are then fed into the standard input of the command. The delimiter tells the shell that the here document has completed. Without it, the shell continues to read input forever. The delimiter must be a single word that does not contain spaces or tabs. Following is the input to the command wc -l to count total number of line –

```
$wc -l << EOF
    This is a simple lookup program
    for good (and bad) restaurants
```

```
            in Cape Town.
EOF
3
$
```

You can use *here document* to print multiple lines using your script as follows –

```
#!/bin/sh

cat << EOF
This is a simple lookup program
for good (and bad) restaurants
in Cape Town.
EOF
```

This produces the following –

```
This is a simple lookup program
for good (and bad) restaurants
in Cape Town.
```

The following script runs a session with the vi text editor and save the input in the file test.txt.

```
#!/bin/sh

filename=test.txt
vi $filename <<EndOfCommands
i
```

```
This file was created automatically from

a shell script

^[

ZZ

EndOfCommands
```

If you run this script with vim acting as vi, then you will likely see this –

```
$ sh test.sh

Vim: Warning: Input is not from a terminal

$
```

After running the script, you should see the following added to the file test.txt –

```
$ cat test.txt

This file was created automatically from

a shell script

$
```

Discard the output

Sometimes you will need to execute a command, but do not want the output displayed on the screen. In such cases you can discard the output by redirecting it to the file /dev/null –

```
$ command > /dev/null
```

Here `command` is the name of the command you want to execute. The file /dev/null is a special file that automatically discards all its input. To discard both output of a command and its error output, use standard redirection to redirect STDERR to STDOUT –

```
$ command > /dev/null 2>&1
```

Here 2 represents STDERR and 1 represents STDOUT. You can display a message on to STDERR by redirecting STDIN into STDERR as follows –

```
$ echo message 1>&2
```

Command	Description
pgm > file	Output of pgm is redirected to file
pgm < file	Program pgm reads its input from file.
pgm >> file	Output of pgm is appended to file.
n > file	Output from stream with descriptor n redirected to file.
n >> file	Output from stream with descriptor n appended to file.
n >& m	Merge output from stream n with stream m.
n <& m	Merge input from stream n with stream m.

<< tag	Standard input comes from here through next tag at start of line.
|	Takes output from one program, or process, and sends it to another.

Redirection Commands

Complete list of commands that can be used for redirection –

Note that file descriptor 0 is normally standard input (STDIN), 1 is standard output (STDOUT), and 2 is standard error output (STDERR)

Chapter Fifteen: UNIX

SHELL FUNCTION

Functions enable you to break down the overall functionality of a script into smaller, logical subsections, which are then called upon to perform their individual tasks when needed. Using functions to perform repetitive tasks is an excellent way to create code reuse. Code reuse is an important part of modern object-oriented programming principles. Shell functions are similar to subroutines, procedures, and functions in other programming languages.

Creating Functions

To declare a function, simply use the following syntax –

```
function_name () {
   list of commands
}
```

The name of your function is function_name, and that is what you will use to call it from elsewhere in your scripts. The function name must be followed by parentheses, which are followed by a list of commands enclosed within braces.

Example

Example using function –

```
#!/bin/sh


# Define your function here
Hello () {
   echo "Hello World"
}


# Invoke your function
Hello
```

Output

```
$./test.sh
Hello World
$
```

Pass Parameters to a Function

You can define a function, which would accept parameters while calling those functions. These parameters would be represented by $1, $2 and so on. The following is an example where we pass two parameters *Zara* and *Ali* and then we capture and print these parameters in the function.

```
#!/bin/sh


# Define your function here
Hello () {
   echo "Hello World $1 $2"
}
```

```
# Invoke your function
Hello Zara Ali
```

Output

```
$./test.sh
Hello World Zara Ali
$
```

Returning Values from Functions

If you execute an exit command from inside a function, its effect is not only to terminate execution of the function but also of the shell program that called the function. If you instead want to just terminate execution of the function, then there is a way to come out of a defined function. Based on the situation you can return any value from your function using the `return` command whose syntax is as follows –

```
return code
```

Here *code* can be anything you choose, but obviously you should choose something that is meaningful or useful in the context of your script as a whole.

Example

Following function returns a value 1 –

```
#!/bin/sh
```

```
# Define your function here
Hello () {
   echo "Hello World $1 $2"
   return 10
}


# Invoke your function
Hello Zara Ali


# Capture value returned by last command
ret=$?


echo "Return value is $ret"
```

Output

```
$./test.sh
Hello World Zara Ali
Return value is 10
$
```

Nested Functions

One of the more interesting features of functions is that they can call themselves as well as call other functions. A function that calls itself is known as a *recursive function*.

The following example demonstrates a nesting of two functions –

```sh
#!/bin/sh

# Calling one function from another
number_one () {
   echo "This is the first function speaking..."
   number_two
}

number_two () {
   echo "This is now the second function speaking..."
}

# Calling function one.
number_one
```

Output

```
This is the first function speaking...
This is now the second function speaking...
```

Function Call from Prompt

You can put definitions for commonly used functions inside your *.profile* so they will be available whenever you log in. Alternatively, you can group the definitions in a file, say *test.sh*, and then execute the file in the current shell by typing –

```
$. test.sh
```

This has the effect of causing any functions defined inside test.sh to be read in and defined to the current shell as follows –

```
$ number_one
This is the first function speaking...
This is now the second function speaking...
$
```

To remove the definition of a function from the shell, you use the unset command with the .f option. This is the same command you use to remove the definition of a variable to the shell.

```
$unset .f function_name
```

Unix - Pipes and Filters

You can connect two commands together so that the output from one program becomes the input of the next program. Two or more commands connected in this way form a pipe. To make a pipe, put a vertical bar (|) on the command line between two commands. When a program takes its input from another program, performs some operation on that input, and writes the result to the standard output, it is referred to as a *filter*.

The grep Command

The grep program searches a file or files for lines that have a certain pattern. The syntax is –

```
$grep pattern file(s)
```

The name "grep" derives from the ed (a UNIX line editor) command g/re/p, which means, "globally search for a regular expression and print all lines containing it." A regular expression is either plain text (a word, for example) and/or special characters used for pattern matching. The simplest use of grep is to look for a pattern consisting of a single word. It can be used in a pipe so that only those lines of the input files containing a given string are sent to the standard output. If you do not give grep a filename to read, it reads its standard input; that is the way all filter programs work –

```
$ls -l | grep "Aug"
-rw-rw-rw-    1 john   doc       11008 Aug  6 14:10 ch02
-rw-rw-rw-    1 john   doc        8515 Aug  6 15:30 ch07
-rw-rw-r--    1 john   doc        2488 Aug 15 10:51 intro
-rw-rw-r--    1 carol  doc        1605 Aug 23 07:35 macros
$
```

Option	Description
-v	Print all lines that do not match pattern.
-n	Print the matched line and its line number.
-l	Print only the names of files with matching lines (letter "l")

-c	Print only the count of matching lines.
-i	Match either upper- or lowercase.

There are various options, which you can use along with grep command –

Next, let's use a regular expression that tells `grep` to find lines with "carol", followed by zero or more other characters abbreviated in a regular expression as ".*"), then followed by "Aug". Here we are using *-i* option to have case insensitive search –

```
$ls -l | grep -i "carol.*aug"
-rw-rw-r--   1 carol doc     1605 Aug 23 07:35 macros
$
```

The sort Command

The `sort` command arranges lines of text alphabetically or numerically. The example below sorts the lines in the food file –

```
$sort food
Afghani Cuisine
Bangkok Wok
Big Apple Deli
Isle of Java
Mandalay
Sushi and Sashimi
```

```
Sweet Tooth

Tio Pepe's Peppers

$
```

The `sort` command arranges lines of text alphabetically by

Option	Description
-n	Sort numerically (example: 10 will sort after 2), ignore blanks and tabs.
-r	Reverse the order of sort.
-f	Sort upper- and lowercase together.
+x	Ignore first x fields when sorting.

default. There are many options that control the sorting –

More than two commands may be linked by a pipe. Taking a previous pipe example using `grep`, we can further sort the files modified in August by order of size.

The following pipe consists of the commands `ls`, `grep,` and `sort` –

```
$ls -l | grep "Aug" | sort +4n

-rw-rw-r--  1 carol doc      1605 Aug 23 07:35 macros

-rw-rw-r--  1 john  doc      2488 Aug 15 10:51 intro

-rw-rw-rw-  1 john  doc      8515 Aug  6 15:30 ch07

-rw-rw-rw-  1 john  doc     11008 Aug  6 14:10 ch02
```

This pipe sorts all files in your directory modified in August by order of size, and prints them to the terminal screen. The sort option +4n skips four fields (fields are separated by blanks) then sort the lines in numeric order.

The pg and more Commands

A long output would normally zip by you on the screen, but if you run text through more or pg as a filter, the display stops after each screen of text. Let us assume that you have a long directory listing. To make it easier to read the sorted listing, pipe the output through more as follows –

```
$ls -l | grep "Aug" | sort +4n | more
-rw-rw-r--  1 carol doc     1605 Aug 23 07:35 macros
-rw-rw-r--  1 john  doc     2488 Aug 15 10:51 intro
-rw-rw-rw-  1 john  doc     8515 Aug  6 15:30 ch07
-rw-rw-r--  1 john  doc    14827 Aug  9 12:40 ch03
                      .
                      .
                      .
-rw-rw-rw-  1 john  doc    16867 Aug  6 15:56 ch05
--More--(74%)
```

The screen will fill up with one screen of text consisting of lines sorted by order of file size. At the bottom of the screen is the more prompt where you can type a command to move through the sorted text. When you are done with this screen, you can use any of the commands listed in the discussion of the `more` program.

Chapter Sixteen: UNIX

USEFUL COMMAND

This quick guide lists commands, including a syntax and brief description. For more detailed information check out commands man page.

```
$man command
```

Files and Directories

These commands allow you to create directories and handle files.

Command	Description
cat	Display File Contents
cd	Changes Directory to dirname
chgrp	Change file group
chmod	Changing Permissions
cp	Copy source file into destination
file	Determine file type
find	Find files
grep	Search files for regular expressions.

head	Display first few lines of a file
ln	Create softlink on oldname
ls	Display information about file type.
mkdir	Create a new directory dirname
more	Display data in paginated form.
mv	Move (Rename) a oldname to newname.
pwd	Print current working directory.
rm	Remove (Delete) filename
rmdir	Delete an existing directory provided it is empty.
tail	Prints last few lines in a file.
touch	Update access and modification time of a file.

Command	Description
awk	Pattern scanning and processing language
cmp	Compare the contents of two files
comm.	Compare sorted data
cut	Cut out selected fields of each line of a file
diff	Differential file comparator
expand	Expand tabs to spaces
join	Join files on some common field
Perl	Data manipulation language
sed	Stream text editor
sort	Sort file data
split	Split file into smaller files
tr	Translate characters
uniq	Report repeated lines in a file
wc	Count words, lines, and characters
vi	Opens vi text editor
vim	Opens vim text editor
fmt	Simple text formatter
spell	Check text for spelling error
ispell	Check text for spelling error
Emacs	GNU project Emacs

ex, edit	Line editor
Emacs	GNU project Emacs

Manipulating data

The contents of files can be compared and altered with the following commands.

Compressed Files

Files may be compressed to save space. Compressed files can be created and examined –

Command	Description
gompress	Compress files
gunzip	Uncompress gzipped files
gzip	GNU alternative compression method
uncompress	Uncompress files
unzip	List, test and extract compressed files in a ZIP archive
zcat	Cat a compressed file
zcmp	Compare compressed files

Command	Description
zdiff	Compare compressed files
zmore	File perusal filter for crt viewing of compressed text

Getting Information

Various Unix manuals and documentation are available on-line. The following Shell commands give information –

Command	Description
apropos	Locate commands by keyword lookup
info	Displays command information pages online
man	Displays manual pages online
whatis	Search the whatis database for complete words.
yelp	GNOME help viewer

Network Communication

The following commands are used to send and receive files from a local UNIX hosts to the remote hosts around the world.

ftp	File transfer program
rcp	Remote file copy
rlogin	Remote login to a UNIX host
rsh	Remote shell
tftp	Trivial file transfer program
telnet	Make terminal connection to another host
ssh	Secure shell terminal or command connection
scp	Secure shell remote file copy
sftp	secure shell file transfer program

Some of these commands may be restricted on your computer for security reasons.

Messages between Users

The UNIX system supports on-screen messaging to other users and worldwide electronic mail –

Command	Description
Evolution	GUI mail handling tool on Linux
mail	Simple send or read mail program
nesg	Permit or deny messages

parcel	Send files to another user
Pine	Vdu-based mail utility
Talk	Talk to another user
write	Write message to another user

Programming Utilities

The following programming tools and languages are available based on which version of Unix you are using

Command	Description
dbx	Sun debugger
gdb	GNU debugger
make	Maintain program groups and compile programs.
nm	Print program's name list
size	Print program's sizes
strip	Remove symbol table and relocation bits
cb	C program beautifier
cc	ANSI C compiler for Suns SPARC systems
Ctrace	C program debugger

Gcc	GNU ANSI C Compiler
Indent	Indent and format C program source
Bc	Interactive arithmetic language processor
Gcl	GNU Common Lisp
Perl	General purpose language
Php	Web page embedded language
Py	Python language interpreter
Asp	Web page embedded language
CC	C++ compiler for Suns SPARC systems
g++	GNU C++ Compiler
Javac	JAVA compiler
appletvieweir	JAVA applet viewer
Netbeans	Java integrated development environment on Linux
Sqlplus	Run the Oracle SQL interpreter
Sqlldr	Run the Oracle SQL data loader
MySql	Run the mysql SQL interpreter

Misc Commands

These commands list or alter system information –

Command	Description
chfn	Change your finger information
chgrp	Change the group ownership of a file
chown	Change owner
date	Print the date
determin	Automatically find terminal type
du	Print amount of disk usage
echo	Echo arguments to the standard options
exit	Quit the system
finger	Print information about logged-in users
groupadd	Create a user group
Show group memberships	
homequota	Show quota and file usage
iostat	Report I/O statistics
kill	Send a signal to a process
last	Show last logins of users
logout	log off UNIX

lun	List user names or login ID
netstat	Show network status
passwd	Change user password
passwd	Change your login password
printenv	Display value of a shell variable
ps	Display the status of current processes
ps	Print process status statistics
quota −v	Display disk usage and limits
reset	Reset terminal mode
script	Keep script of terminal session
script	Save the output of a command or process
setenv	Set environment variables
sty	Set terminal options
time	Time a command
top	Display all system processes
tset	Set terminal mode
tty	Print current terminal name
umask	Show the permissions that are given to view files by default
uname	Display name of the current system

uptime	Get the system up time
useradd	Create a user account
users	Print names of logged in users
vmstat	Report virtual memory statistics
w	Show what logged in users are doing
who	List logged in users

td>groups

Chapter Seventeen:

REGULAR EXPRESSION

A regular expression is a string that can be used to describe several sequences of characters. Regular expressions are used by several different Unix commands, including ed, sed, awk, grep, and, to a more limited extent, vi. Here sed stands for **st**ream **ed**itor a stream oriented editor, which was created exclusively for executing scripts. Thus, all the input you feed into it passes through and goes to STDOUT and it does not change the input file.

Invoking sed

Before we start, let us take make sure you have a local copy of /etc/passwd text file to work with sed. As mentioned previously, sed can be invoked by sending data through a pipe to it as follows –

```
$ cat /etc/passwd | sed
Usage: sed [OPTION]... {script-other-script} [input-file]...

  -n, --quiet, --silent

              suppress automatic printing of pattern space
  -e script, --expression=script

. . . . . . . . . . . . . . . . . . . . . . . . . . . . . .
```

The `cat` command dumps the contents of /etc/passwd to `sed` through the pipe into sed's pattern space. The pattern space is the internal work buffer that `sed` uses to do its work.

The sed General Syntax

General syntax for sed

```
/pattern/action
```

Here, **pattern** is a regular expression, and **action** is one of the commands given in the following table. If **pattern** is omitted, **action** is performed for every line as we have seen above.

The slash characters (/) that surround the pattern are required because they are used as delimiters.

Range	Description
P	Prints the line
D	Deletes the line
s/pattern1/pattern2/	Substitutes the first occurrence of pattern1 with pattern2.

Deleting All Lines with sed

Invoke `sed` again, but this time tell `sed` to use the editing command delete line, denoted by the single letter d –

```
$ cat /etc/passwd | sed 'd'
```

```
$
```

Instead of invoking `sed` by sending a file to it through a pipe, you can instruct `sed` to read the data from a file, as in the following example. The following command does exactly the same thing as the previous example, without the cat command –

```
$ sed -e 'd' /etc/passwd
$
```

The sed Addresses

`sed` also understands something called addresses. Addresses are either particular locations in a file or a range where a particular editing command should be applied. When `sed` encounters no addresses, it performs its operations on every line in the file.

The following command adds a basic address to the `sed` command you have been using –

```
$ cat /etc/passwd | sed '1d' |more
daemon:x:1:1:daemon:/usr/sbin:/bin/sh
bin:x:2:2:bin:/bin:/bin/sh
sys:x:3:3:sys:/dev:/bin/sh
```

```
sync:x:4:65534:sync:/bin:/bin/sync

games:x:5:60:games:/usr/games:/bin/sh

man:x:6:12:man:/var/cache/man:/bin/sh

mail:x:8:8:mail:/var/mail:/bin/sh

news:x:9:9:news:/var/spool/news:/bin/sh

backup:x:34:34:backup:/var/backups:/bin/sh

$
```

Notice that the number 1 is added before the delete edit command. This tells `sed` to perform the editing command on the first line of the file. In this example, `sed` will delete the first line of /etc/password and print the rest of the file.

The sed Address Ranges

So, what if you want to remove more than one line from a file? You can specify an address range with `sed` as follows –

```
$ cat /etc/passwd | sed '1, 5d' |more

games:x:5:60:games:/usr/games:/bin/sh

man:x:6:12:man:/var/cache/man:/bin/sh

mail:x:8:8:mail:/var/mail:/bin/sh

news:x:9:9:news:/var/spool/news:/bin/sh

backup:x:34:34:backup:/var/backups:/bin/sh

$
```

The above command will be applied on all the lines starting from 1 through 5. Therefore, it deletes the first five lines.

Try out the following address ranges –

Range	Description
'4,10d'	Lines starting from 4th till 10th are deleted
'10,4d'	Only 10th line is deleted, because sed does not work in reverse direction.
'4,+5d'	This will match line 4 in the file, delete that line, continue to delete the next five lines, and then cease its deletion and print the rest
'2,5!d'	This will deleted everything except starting from 2nd till 5th line.
'1~3d'	This deletes the first line, steps over the next three lines, and then deletes the fourth line. Sed continues applying this pattern until the end of the file.
'2~2d'	This tells sed to delete the second line, step over the next line, delete the next line, and repeat until the end of the file is reached.
'4,10p'	Lines starting from 4th till 10th are printed
'4,d'	This would generate syntax error.
',10d'	This would also generate syntax error.

Note: While using p action, you should use -n option to avoid repetition of line printing. Check the difference between these two commands –

```
$ cat /etc/passwd | sed -n '1,3p'
```

Check the above command without –n as follows –

```
$ cat /etc/passwd | sed '1,3p'
```

The Substitution Command

The substitution command, denoted by s, will substitute any string that you specify with any other string that you specify. To substitute one string with another, you need to have a way of telling sed where your first string ends and the substitution string begins. This is traditionally done by bookending the two strings with the forward slash (/) character. The following command substitutes the first occurrence on a line of the string **root** with the string **amrood**.

```
$ cat /etc/passwd | sed 's/root/amrood/'
amrood:x:0:0:root user:/root:/bin/sh
daemon:x:1:1:daemon:/usr/sbin:/bin/sh
. . . . . . . . . . . . . . . . . . . . . . . .
```

It is very important to note that sed substitutes only the first occurrence on a line. If the string root occurs more than once on a line, only the first match will be replaced. To tell sed to do a global substitution, add the letter g to the end of the command as follows –

```
$ cat /etc/passwd | sed 's/root/amrood/g'
```

```
amrood:x:0:0:amrood user:/amrood:/bin/sh

daemon:x:1:1:daemon:/usr/sbin:/bin/sh

bin:x:2:2:bin:/bin:/bin/sh

sys:x:3:3:sys:/dev:/bin/sh

. . . . . . . . . . . . . . . . . . . . . . . . . . .
```

Substitution Flags

There are a number of other useful flags that can be passed in addition to the g flag, and you can specify more than one at a

Flag	Description
g	Replace all matches, not just the first match.
NUMBER	Replace only NUMBERth match.
p	If substitution was made, print pattern space.
w FILENAME	If substitution was made, write result to FILENAME.
I or i	Match in a case-insensitive manner.
M or m	In addition to the normal behavior of the special regular expression characters ^ and $, this flag causes ^ to match the empty string after a newline and $ to match the empty string before a newline.

time.

Using an Alternative String Separator

You may find yourself having to do a substitution on a string that includes the forward slash character. In this case, you can specify a different separator by providing the designated character after the s.

```
$ cat /etc/passwd | sed 's:/root:/amrood:g'
amrood:x:0:0:amrood user:/amrood:/bin/sh
daemon:x:1:1:daemon:/usr/sbin:/bin/sh
```

In the above example we used: as delimiter instead of slash / because we were trying to search /root instead of simple root.

Replacing with Empty Space

Use an empty substitution string to delete the root string from the /etc/passwd file entirely –

```
$ cat /etc/passwd | sed 's/root//g'
:x:0:0::/:/bin/sh
daemon:x:1:1:daemon:/usr/sbin:/bin/sh
```

Address Substitution

If you want to substitute the string 'sh' with the string 'quiet' on line 10, you can specify it as follows –

```
$ cat /etc/passwd | sed '10s/sh/quiet/g'
root:x:0:0:root user:/root:/bin/sh
```

```
daemon:x:1:1:daemon:/usr/sbin:/bin/sh

bin:x:2:2:bin:/bin:/bin/sh

sys:x:3:3:sys:/dev:/bin/sh

sync:x:4:65534:sync:/bin:/bin/sync

games:x:5:60:games:/usr/games:/bin/sh

man:x:6:12:man:/var/cache/man:/bin/sh

mail:x:8:8:mail:/var/mail:/bin/sh

news:x:9:9:news:/var/spool/news:/bin/sh

backup:x:34:34:backup:/var/backups:/bin/quiet
```

Similarly, to do an address range substitution, you could do something like this –

```
$ cat /etc/passwd | sed '1,5s/sh/quiet/g'

root:x:0:0:root user:/root:/bin/quiet

daemon:x:1:1:daemon:/usr/sbin:/bin/quiet

bin:x:2:2:bin:/bin:/bin/quiet

sys:x:3:3:sys:/dev:/bin/quiet

sync:x:4:65534:sync:/bin:/bin/sync

games:x:5:60:games:/usr/games:/bin/sh

man:x:6:12:man:/var/cache/man:/bin/sh

mail:x:8:8:mail:/var/mail:/bin/sh

news:x:9:9:news:/var/spool/news:/bin/sh

backup:x:34:34:backup:/var/backups:/bin/sh
```

As you can see from the output, the first five lines had the string 'sh' changed to 'quiet,' but the rest of the lines were left untouched.

The Matching Command

You would use p option along with −n option to print all the matching lines as follows −

```
$ cat testing | sed -n '/root/p'
root:x:0:0:root user:/root:/bin/sh
[root@ip-72-167-112-17 amrood]# vi testing
root:x:0:0:root user:/root:/bin/sh
daemon:x:1:1:daemon:/usr/sbin:/bin/sh
bin:x:2:2:bin:/bin:/bin/sh
sys:x:3:3:sys:/dev:/bin/sh
sync:x:4:65534:sync:/bin:/bin/sync
games:x:5:60:games:/usr/games:/bin/sh
man:x:6:12:man:/var/cache/man:/bin/sh
mail:x:8:8:mail:/var/mail:/bin/sh
news:x:9:9:news:/var/spool/news:/bin/sh
backup:x:34:34:backup:/var/backups:/bin/sh
```

Using Regular Expression

While matching patterns, you can use regular expressions, which provide greater flexibility. Check the following example, which matches all the lines starting with *daemon* and then deletes them −

```
$ cat testing | sed '/^daemon/d'
root:x:0:0:root user:/root:/bin/sh
bin:x:2:2:bin:/bin:/bin/sh
sys:x:3:3:sys:/dev:/bin/sh
```

```
sync:x:4:65534:sync:/bin:/bin/sync

games:x:5:60:games:/usr/games:/bin/sh

man:x:6:12:man:/var/cache/man:/bin/sh

mail:x:8:8:mail:/var/mail:/bin/sh

news:x:9:9:news:/var/spool/news:/bin/sh

backup:x:34:34:backup:/var/backups:/bin/sh
```

Example that deletes all lines ending with **sh** –

```
$ cat testing | sed '/sh$/d'

sync:x:4:65534:sync:/bin:/bin/sync
```

The following table lists four special characters that are very useful in regular expressions.

Character	Description
^	Matches the beginning of lines.
$	Matches the end of lines.
.	Matches any single character.
*	Matches zero or more occurrences of the previous character
[chars]	Matches any one of the characters given in chars, where chars is a sequence of characters. You can use the - character to indicate a range of characters.

Matching Characters

Expression	Description
/a.c/	Matches lines that contain strings such as a+c, a-c, abc, match, and a3c, whereas the pattern
/a*c/	Matches the same strings along with strings such as ace, yacc, and arctic.
/[tT]he/	Matches the string The and the:
/^$/	Matches Blank lines
/^.*$/	Matches an entire line whatever it is.
/ */	Matches one or more spaces
/^$/	Matches Blank lines

Expressions to demonstrate the use of metacharacters.

Set	Description
[a-z]	Matches a single lowercase letter
[A-Z]	Matches a single uppercase letter
[a-zA-Z]	Matches a single letter
[0-9]	Matches a single number

[a-zA-Zo-9]	Matches a single letter or number

The following table shows some frequently used sets of characters –

Character Class Keywords

Some special keywords are commonly available to regexps, especially GNU utilities that employ regexps. These are very useful for sed regular expressions as they simplify things and enhance readability.

For example, the characters a through z as well as the characters A through Z constitute one such class of characters that has the keyword [[:alpha:]] Using the alphabet character class keyword, this command prints only those lines in the /etc/syslog.conf file that start with a letter of the alphabet –

```
$ cat /etc/syslog.conf | sed -n '/^[[:alpha:]]/p'
authpriv.*                      /var/log/secure
mail.*                          -/var/log/maillog
cron.*                          /var/log/cron
uucp,news.crit                  /var/log/spooler
local7.*                        /var/log/boot.log
```

Character Class	Description

[[:alnum:]]	Alphanumeric [a-z A-Z 0-9]
[[:alpha:]]	Alphabetic [a-z A-Z]
[[:blank:]]	Blank characters (spaces or tabs)
[[:cntrl:]]	Control characters
[[:digit:]]	Numbers [0-9]
[[:graph:]]	Any visible characters (excludes whitespace)
[[:lower:]]	Lowercase letters [a-z]
[[:print:]]	Printable characters (noncontrol characters)
[[:punct:]]	Punctuation characters
[[:space:]]	Whitespace
[[:upper:]]	Uppercase letters [A-Z]
[[:xdigit:]]	Hex digits [0-9 a-f A-F]

C omplete list of available character class keywords in GNU sed.

Ampersand Referencing

The sed metacharacter & represents the contents of the pattern that was matched. For instance, you have a file called phone.txt full of phone numbers –

```
5555551212

5555551213
```

```
5555551214

6665551215

6665551216

7775551217
```

You want to make the area code (the first three digits) surrounded by parentheses for easier reading. To do this, you can use the ampersand replacement character, like so –

```
$ sed -e 's/^[[:digit:]][[:digit:]][[:digit:]]/(&)/g' phone.txt
(555)5551212
(555)5551213
(555)5551214
(666)5551215
(666)5551216
(777)5551217
```

Here you are matching the first 3 digits and then using & replacing those 3 digits with surrounding parentheses.

Using Multiple sed Commands

You can use multiple `sed` commands in a single `sed` command as follows –

```
$ sed -e 'command1' -e 'command2' ... -e 'commandN' files
```

Here command1 through commandN are `sed` commands of the type discussed previously. These commands are applied to each line in the list of files given by files. Using the same mechanism, we can write above phone number example as follows –

```
$ sed -e 's/^[[:digit:]]\{3\}/(&)/g' \
                    -e 's/)[[:digit:]]\{3\}/&-/g' phone.txt
(555)555-1212
(555)555-1213
(555)555-1214
(666)555-1215
(666)555-1216
(777)555-1217
```

Note – In the above example, instead of repeating the character class keyword [[:digit:]] three times, you replaced it with \{3\}, which means to match the preceding regular expression three times. Here I used \ to give line break you should remove this before running this command.

Back References

The ampersand metacharacter is useful, but even more useful is the ability to define specific regions in a regular expression so you can reference them in your replacement strings. By defining specific parts of a regular expression, you can then refer back to those parts with a special reference character. To do back references, you have to first define a region and then refer back to that region. To define a region you insert backslash parentheses around each region of interest. The first region that you surround with backslashes is then referenced by \1, the second region by \2, and so on.

Assuming phone.txt has the following text –

```
(555)555-1212
(555)555-1213
(555)555-1214
(666)555-1215
(666)555-1216
(777)555-1217
```

Now try the following command –

```
$ cat phone.txt | sed 's/\(.*)\)\(.*-\)\(.*$\)/Area \
                 code: \1 Second: \2 Third: \3/'
Area code: (555) Second: 555- Third: 1212
Area code: (555) Second: 555- Third: 1213
Area code: (555) Second: 555- Third: 1214
Area code: (666) Second: 555- Third: 1215
Area code: (666) Second: 555- Third: 1216
Area code: (777) Second: 555- Third: 1217
```

Note: In the above example each regular expression inside the parenthesis would be back referenced by \1, \2 and so on. Here I used \ to give line break you should remove this before running this command.

Chapter Eighteen: FILE SYSTEM BASICS

A file system is a logical collection of files on a partition or disk. A partition is a container for information and can span an entire hard drive if desired. Your hard drive can have various partitions which usually contain only one file system, such as one file system housing the / file system or another containing the /home file system. One file system per partition allows for the logical maintenance and management of differing file systems. Everything in Unix is considered to be a file, including physical devices such as DVD-ROMs, USB devices, floppy drives, and so forth.

Directory Structure

Unix uses a hierarchical file system structure, much like an upside-down tree, with root (/) at the base of the file system and all other directories spreading from there. A UNIX file system is a collection of files and directories that have the following properties –

- It has a root directory (/) that contains other files and directories.

- Each file or directory is uniquely identified by its name, the directory in which it resides, and a unique identifier, typically called an inode.

- By convention, the root directory has an inode number of 2 and the lost+found directory has an inode number of 3. Inode numbers 0 and 1 are not used. File inode numbers can be seen by specifying the `-i` option to `ls` command.

- It is self-contained. There are no dependencies between one file system and any other.

The directories have specific purposes and generally hold the same types of information for easily locating files. The following are the directories that exist on the major versions of Unix –

Directory	Description
/	This is the root directory, which should contain only the directories needed at the top level of the file structure.
/bin	This is where the executable files are located. They are available to all users.
/dev	These are device drivers.
/etc	Supervisor directory commands, configuration files, disk configuration files, valid user lists, groups, ethernet, hosts, where to send critical messages.
/lib	Contains shared library files and sometimes other kernel-related files.

/boot	Contains files for booting the system.
/home	Contains the home directory for users and other accounts.
/mnt	Used to mount other temporary file systems, such as cdrom and floppy for the CD-ROM drive and floppy diskette drive, respectively.
/proc	Contains all processes marked as a file by process number or other information that is dynamic to the system.
/tmp	Holds temporary files used between system boots.
/usr	Used for miscellaneous purposes, can be used by many users. Includes administrative commands, shared files, library files, and others.
/var	Typically contains variable-length files such as log and print files and other file types that may contain a variable amount of data.
/sbin	Contains binary (executable) files, usually for system administration. For example *fdisk* and *ifconfig* utlities.
/kernel	Contains kernel files

Navigating the File System

Now that you understand the basics of the file system, you can begin navigating to the files you need. The following are commands you will use to navigate the system –

Command	Description
cat filename	Displays a filename.
cd dirname	Moves you to the directory identified.
cp file1 file2	Copies one file/directory to specified location.
file filename	Identifies the file type (binary, text, etc).
find filename dir	Finds a file/directory.
head filename	Shows the beginning of a file.
less filename	Browses through a file from end or beginning.
ls dirname	Shows the contents of the directory specified.
mkdir dirname	Creates the specified directory.

Command	Description
more filename	Browses through a file from beginning to end.
mv file1 file2	Moves the location of or renames a file/directory.
pwd	Shows the current directory the user is in.
rm filename	Removes a file.
rmdir dirname	Removes a directory.
tail filename	Shows the end of a file.
touch filename	Creates a blank file or modifies an existing file.s attributes.
whereis filename	Shows the location of a file.
which filename	Shows the location of a file if it is in your PATH.

You can use **Manpage Help** to check complete syntax for each of these commands.

The df Command

The first way to manage your partition space is with the `df`
(disk free) command. The command `df -k` (disk free)
displays the disk space usage in kilobytes, as shown below –

```
$df -k

Filesystem       1K-blocks       Used    Available Use% Mounted on

/dev/vzfs        10485760    7836644     2649116  75% /

/devices                0          0           0   0% /devices

$
```

Some of the directories, such as /devices, shows 0 in the
kbytes, used, and avail columns as well as 0% for capacity.
These are special (or virtual) file systems, and although they
reside on the disk under /, by themselves they do not take up
disk space.

The `df -k` output is generally the same on all Unix systems.
Here's what it usually includes –

Column	Description
Filesystem	The physical file system name.
Kbytes	Total kilobytes of space available on

	the storage medium.
Used	Total kilobytes of space used (by files).
Avail	Total kilobytes available for use.
Capacity	Percentage of total space used by files.
Mounted on	What the file system is mounted on.

You can use the -h (human readable) option to display the output in a format that shows the size in easier-to-understand notation.

The du Command

The du (disk usage) command enables you to specify directories to show disk space usage on a particular directory. This command is helpful if you want to determine how much space a particular directory is using. The following command will display the number of blocks used by each directory. A single block may take either 512 Bytes or 1 Kilo Byte depending on your system.

```
$du /etc
10       /etc/cron.d
126      /etc/default
6        /etc/dfs
...
$
```

The −h option makes the output easier to comprehend −

```
$du -h /etc

5k    /etc/cron.d

63k   /etc/default

3k    /etc/dfs

...

$
```

Mounting the File System

A file system must be mounted in order to be usable by the system. To see what is currently mounted (available for use) on your system, use this command −

```
$ mount
/dev/vzfs on / type reiserfs (rw,usrquota,grpquota)
proc on /proc type proc (rw,nodiratime)
devpts on /dev/pts type devpts (rw)
$
```

The /mnt directory, by Unix convention, is where temporary mounts (such as CD-ROM drives, remote network drives, and floppy drives) are located. If you need to mount a file system, you can use the mount command with the following syntax −

```
mount -t file_system_type device_to_mount directory_to_mount_to
```

For example, if you want to mount a CD-ROM to the directory /mnt/cdrom, for example, you can type −

```
$ mount -t iso9660 /dev/cdrom /mnt/cdrom
```

This assumes that your CD-ROM device is called /dev/cdrom
and that you want to mount it to /mnt/cdrom. Refer to the
mount man page for more specific information or type mount
-h at the command line for help information. After mounting,
you can use the cd command to navigate the newly available
file system through the mountpoint you just created.

Unmounting the File System

To unmount (remove) the file system from your system, use
the umount command by identifying the mountpoint or
device. For example, to unmount cdrom, use the following
command –

```
$ umount /dev/cdrom
```

The mount command enables you to access your file systems,
but on most modern Unix systems, the automount function
makes this process invisible to the user and requires no
intervention.

User and Group Quotas

User and group quotas provide the mechanisms by which the
amount of space used by a single user or all users within a
specific group can be limited to a value defined by the
administrator. Quotas operate around two limits that allow
the user to take some action if the amount of space, or

number of disk blocks start to reach the administrator defined limits –

- **Soft Limit** – If the user exceeds the limit defined, there is a grace period that allows the user to free up some space.

- **Hard Limit** – When the hard limit is reached, regardless of the grace period, no further files or blocks can be allocated.

There are a number of commands to administer quotas –

Command	Description
quota	Displays disk usage and limits for a user of group.
edquota	This is a quota editor. Users or Groups quota can be edited using this command.
quotacheck	Scan a file system for disk usage, create, check and repair quota files
setquota	This is also a command line quota editor.
quotaon	This announces to the system that disk quotas should be enabled on one or more file systems.
quotaoff	This announces to the system that disk quotas should be disabled off one or more file systems.
repquota	This prints a summary of the disc usage and quotas for the specified file systems

Chapter Nineteen:

UNIX-USER ADMINISTRATION

There are three types of accounts on Unix system –

- **Root account** – also called superuser and has complete and unfettered control of the system. A superuser can run any commands without any restriction. This user should be assumed as a system administrator.

- **System accounts** – System accounts are those needed for the operation of system-specific components for example mail accounts and the sshd accounts. These accounts are usually needed for some specific function on your system, and any modifications to them could adversely affect the system.

- **User accounts** – User accounts provide interactive access to the system for users and groups of users. General users are typically assigned to these accounts and usually have limited access to critical system files and directories.

UNIX supports a concept of *Group Account* , which logically groups a number of accounts. Every account would be a part of any group account. Unix groups plays important role in handling file permissions and process management.

Managing Users and Groups

There are three main user administration files –

- **/etc/passwd:** – Keeps user account and password information. This file holds the majority of information about accounts on the Unix system.

- **/etc/shadow:** – Holds the encrypted password of the corresponding account. Not all systems support this file.

- **/etc/group:** – Contains group information for each account.

- **/etc/gshadow:** – Contains secure group account information.

Check all the above files using `cat` command.

Commands available on the majority of Unix systems to create and manage accounts and groups –

Command	Description
useradd	Adds accounts to the system.
usermod	Modifies account attributes.
userdel	Deletes accounts from the system.
groupadd	Adds groups to the system.
groupmod	Modifies group attributes.
groupdel	Removes groups from the system.

Create a Group

You need to create groups before creating any account otherwise you would have to use existing groups on your system. You have all the groups listed in */etc/groups* file. All the default groups would be system account specific groups and it is not recommended to use them for ordinary accounts. Use the following syntax to create a new group account –

```
groupadd [-g gid [-o]] [-r] [-f] groupname
```

Here are the details of the parameters:

Option	Description
-g GID	The numerical value of the group's ID.
-o	This option permits to add group with non-unique GID

-r	This flag instructs groupadd to add a system account
-f	This option causes to just exit with success status if the specified group already exists. With -g, if specified GID already exists, other (unique) GID is chosen
groupname	Actual group name to be created.

If you do not specify any parameters then the system will use the default values.

The following example will create a *developers* group with default values, which is acceptable for most administrators.

```
$ groupadd developers
```

Modify a Group

To modify a group, use the `groupmod` syntax –

```
$ groupmod -n new_modified_group_name old_group_name
```

To change the developers_2 group name to developer, type –

```
$ groupmod -n developer developer_2
```

Here is how you would change the financial GID to 545 –

```
$ groupmod -g 545 developer
```

Delete a Group:

To delete an existing group, all you need are the `groupdel` command and the group name. To delete the developer group, the command is –

```
$ groupdel developer
```

This removes only the group, not any files associated with that group. The files are still accessible by their owners.

Create an Account

Let us see how to create a new account on your Unix system. Use the syntax to create a user's account –

```
useradd -d homedir -g groupname -m -s shell -u userid accountname
```

Available Parameters –

Option	Description
-d homedir	Specifies home directory for the account.
-g groupname	Specifies a group account for this account.
-m	Creates the home directory if it doesn't exist.
-s shell	Specifies the default shell for this account.

-u userid   You can specify a user id for this account.

accountname   Actual account name to be created

If you do not specify a parameter then system will use the default values. The `useradd` command modifies the /etc/passwd, /etc/shadow, and /etc/group files and creates a home directory. The following is an example which will create an account *mcmohd* setting its home directory to */home/mcmohd* and group as *developers*. This user would have Korn Shell assigned to it.

```
$ useradd -d /home/mcmohd -g developers -s /bin/ksh mcmohd
```

Before issuing the above command, make sure you already have a *developers* group created using *groupadd* command. Once an account is created you can set its password using the **passwd** command as follows –

```
$ passwd mcmohd20
Changing password for user mcmohd20.
New UNIX password:
Retype new UNIX password:
passwd: all authentication tokens updated successfully.
```

When you type *passwd accountname*, it gives you option to change the password provided you are superuser otherwise you would be able to change just your password using the same command but without specifying your account name.

Modify an Account

The `usermod` command enables you to make changes to an existing account from the command line. It uses the same arguments as the `useradd` command, plus the `-l` argument, which allows you to change the account name. For example, to change the account name *mcmohd* to *mcmohd20* and to change home directory accordingly, you would need to issue following command –

```
$ usermod -d /home/mcmohd20 -m -l mcmohd mcmohd20
```

Delete an Account

The `userdel` command can be used to delete an existing user. This is a very dangerous command if not used with caution. There is only one argument or option available for the command: `-r`, for removing the account's home directory and mail file. For example, to remove account *mcmohd20*, you would need to issue following command –

```
$ userdel -r mcmohd20
```

If you want to keep the home directory for backup purposes, omit the `-r` option. You can remove the home directory as needed at a later time.

Chapter Twenty: SYSTEM PERFORMANCE

The purpose of this tutorial is to introduce the performance analyst to some of the free tools available to monitor and manage performance on UNIX systems, and to provide a guideline on how to diagnose and fix performance problems in a Unix environment. UNIX has following major resource types that need to be monitored and tuned –

- CPU
- Memory
- Disk space
- Communications lines
- I/O Time
- Network Time
- Applications programs

Performance Components

There are five major components where total system time goes –

Component	Description
User state CPU	The actual amount of time the CPU spends running the users program in the user state. It includes time spent executing library calls, but does not include time spent in the kernel on its behalf.
System state CPU	This is the amount of time the CPU spends in the system state on behalf of this program. All I/O routines require kernel services. The programmer can affect this value by the use of blocking for I/O transfers.
I/O Time and Network Time	These are the amount of time spent moving data and servicing I/O requests
Virtual Memory Performance	This includes context switching and swapping.
Application Program	Time spent running other programs - when the system is not servicing this application because another application currently has the CPU.

Command	Description
nice/renice	Run a program with modified scheduling priority
netstat	Print network connections, routing tables, interface statistics, masquerade connections, and multicast memberships
time	Time a simple command or give resource usage
uptime	System Load Average
ps	Report a snapshot of the current processes.
vmstat	Report virtual memory statistics
gprof	Display call graph profile data
prof	Process Profiling
top	Display system tasks

Performance Tools

Unix provides the following important tools to measure and fine-tune Unix system performance –

Unix - System Logging

UNIX systems have a very flexible and powerful logging system, which enables you to record almost anything and then manipulate the logs to retrieve the information you require. Many versions of UNIX provide a general-purpose logging facility called syslog. Individual programs that need to have information logged send the information to syslog.

Unix syslog is a host-configurable, uniform system logging facility. The system uses a centralized system logging process that runs the program **/etc/syslogd** or **/etc/syslog**.

The operation of the system logger is quite straightforward. Programs send their log entries to syslogd, which consults the configuration file /etc/syslogd.conf or /etc/syslog and, when a match is found, writes the log message to the desired log file.

Term	Description
Facility	The identifier used to describe the application or process that submitted the log message. Examples are mail, kernel, and ftp.
Priority	An indicator of the importance of the message. Levels are defined within syslog as guidelines, from debugging information to critical events.
Selector	A combination of one or more facilities and levels. When an incoming event matches a selector, an action is performed.

| Action | What happens to an incoming message that matches a selector. Actions can write the message to a log file, echo the message to a console or other device, write the message to a logged in user, or send the message along to another syslog server. |

There are four basic syslog terms that you should understand –

Syslog Facilities

Facility	Description
auth	Activity related to requesting name and password (getty, su, login).
authpriv	Same as auth but logged to a file that can only be read by selected users.
console	Used to capture messages that would generally be directed to the system console.
cron	Messages from the cron system scheduler.
daemon	System daemon catchall.
ftp	Messages relating to the ftp daemon.
kern	Kernel messages.

local0.local7	Local facilities defined per site.
lpr	Messages from the line printing system.
mail	Messages relating to the mail system.
mark	Pseudo-event used to generate timestamps in log files.
news	Messages relating to network news protocol (nntp).
ntp	Messages relating to network time protocol.
user	Regular user processes.
uucp	UUCP subsystem.

Here are the available facilities for the selector. Not all facilities are present on all versions of UNIX.

Syslog Priorities

Priority	Description
emerg	Emergency condition, such as an imminent system crash, usually broadcast to all users.
alert	Condition that should be corrected immediately, such as a corrupted system database.

crit	Critical condition, such as a hardware error.
err	Ordinary error.
warning	Warning.
notice	Condition that is not an error, but possibly should be handled in a special way.
info	Informational message.
debug	Messages that are used when debugging programs.
none	Pseudo level used to specify not to log messages.

The syslog priorities are summarized in the following table –

The combination of facilities and levels enables you to be discerning about what is logged and where that information goes. As each program sends its messages dutifully to the system logger, the logger makes decisions on what to keep track of and what to discard based on the levels defined in the selector. When you specify a level, the system will keep track of everything at that level and higher.

The /etc/syslog.conf file

The /etc/syslog.conf file controls where messages are logged. A typical syslog.conf file might look like this –

```
*.err;kern.debug;auth.notice /dev/console
```

```
daemon,auth.notice          /var/log/messages

lpr.info                    /var/log/lpr.log

mail.*                      /var/log/mail.log

ftp.*                       /var/log/ftp.log

auth.*                      @prep.ai.mit.edu

auth.*                      root,amrood

netinfo.err                 /var/log/netinfo.log

install.*                   /var/log/install.log

*.emerg                     *

*.alert                     |program_name

mark.*                      /dev/console
```

Each line of the file contains two parts –

- A message selector that specifies which kind of messages to log. For example, all error messages or all debugging messages from the kernel.

- An action field that says what should be done with the message. For example, put it in a file or send the message to a user's terminal.

Following are the notable points for the above configuration –

- Message selectors have two parts: a facility and a priority. For example,*kern.debug* selects all debug messages (the priority) generated by the kernel (the facility).

- Message selector *kern.debug* selects all priorities that are greater than debug.

- An asterisk in place of either the facility or the priority indicates "all." For example, *.debug means all debug messages, while kern.* means all messages generated by the kernel.

- You can also use commas to specify multiple facilities. Two or more selectors can be grouped together by using a semicolon.

Logging Actions

The action field specifies one of five actions –

- Log messages to a file or a device. For example, /var/log/lpr.log or /dev/console.

- Send a message to a user. You can specify multiple usernames by separating them with commas (e.g., root, amrood).

- Send a message to all users. In this case, the action field consists of an asterisk (e.g., *).

- Pipe the message to a program. In this case, the program is specified after the UNIX pipe symbol (|).

- Send the message to the syslog on another host. In this case, the action field consists of a hostname, preceded by an at sign (e.g., @tutorialspoint.com)

The logger Command

UNIX provides the `logger` command, which is extremely useful for system logging. The `logger` command sends logging messages to the syslogd daemon, and consequently provokes system logging. This means we can check from the command line at any time using the `syslogd` daemon and its configuration. The `logger` command provides a method for adding one-line entries to the system log file from the command line.

The format of the command is –

logger [-i] [-f file] [-p priority] [-t tag] [message]...

Here is the detail of the parameters –

Option	Description
-f filename	Use the contents of file filename as the message to log.
-i	Log the process ID of the logger process with each line.
-p priority	Enter the message with the specified priority (specified selector entry); the message priority can be specified numerically, or as a facility.priority pair. The default priority is user.notice.
-t tag	Mark each line added to the log with the specified tag.

message	The string arguments whose contents are concatenated together in the specified order, separated by the space

You can use **Manpage Help** to check complete syntax for this command.

Log Rotation

Log files have the propensity to grow very fast and consume large amounts of disk space. To enable log rotations, most distributions use tools such as *newsyslog* or *logrotate*. These tools should be called at frequent intervals using the cron daemon. Check the man pages for *newsyslog* or *logrotate* for more details.

Important Log Locations

All the system applications create their log files in */var/log* and its sub-directories. Here are few important

Application	Directory
httpd	/var/log/httpd
samba	/var/log/samba
cron	/var/log/
mail	/var/log/
mysql	/var/log/

applications and their corresponding log directories –

Chapter Twenty-one:

UNIX SIGNALS AND TRAPS

Signals are software interrupts sent to a program to indicate that an important event has occurred. The events can vary from user requests to illegal memory access errors. Some signals, such as the interrupt signal, indicate that a user has asked the program to do something that is not in the usual flow of control.

The following are some of the more common signals you might encounter and want to use in your programs –

Signal Name	Signal Number	Description
SIGHUP	1	Hang up detected on controlling terminal or death of controlling process
SIGINT	2	Issued if the user sends an interrupt signal (Ctrl + C).
SIGQUIT	3	Issued if the user sends a quit signal (Ctrl + D).
SIGFPE	8	Issued if an illegal mathematical operation is attempted
SIGKILL	9	If a process gets this signal it must quit immediately and will not perform any

	cleanup operations	
SIGALRM 14	Alarm Clock signal (used for timers)	
SIGTERM 15	Software termination signal (sent by kill by default).	

LIST of Signals

There is an easy way to list all the signals supported by your system. Just issue the `kill -l` command and it will display all the supported signals –

```
$ kill -l
 1) SIGHUP       2) SIGINT      3) SIGQUIT     4) SIGILL
 5) SIGTRAP      6) SIGABRT     7) SIGBUS      8) SIGFPE
 9) SIGKILL     10) SIGUSR1    11) SIGSEGV    12) SIGUSR2
13) SIGPIPE     14) SIGALRM    15) SIGTERM    16) SIGSTKFLT
17) SIGCHLD     18) SIGCONT    19) SIGSTOP    20) SIGTSTP
21) SIGTTIN     22) SIGTTOU    23) SIGURG     24) SIGXCPU
25) SIGXFSZ     26) SIGVTALRM  27) SIGPROF    28) SIGWINCH
29) SIGIO       30) SIGPWR     31) SIGSYS     34) SIGRTMIN
35) SIGRTMIN+1  36) SIGRTMIN+2 37) SIGRTMIN+3 38) SIGRTMIN+4
39) SIGRTMIN+5  40) SIGRTMIN+6 41) SIGRTMIN+7 42) SIGRTMIN+8
43) SIGRTMIN+9  44) SIGRTMIN+10 45) SIGRTMIN+11 46) SIGRTMIN+12
47) SIGRTMIN+13 48) SIGRTMIN+14 49) SIGRTMIN+15 50) SIGRTMAX-14
51) SIGRTMAX-13 52) SIGRTMAX-12 53) SIGRTMAX-11 54) SIGRTMAX-10
55) SIGRTMAX-9  56) SIGRTMAX-8  57) SIGRTMAX-7  58) SIGRTMAX-6
59) SIGRTMAX-5  60) SIGRTMAX-4  61) SIGRTMAX-3  62) SIGRTMAX-2
63) SIGRTMAX-1  64) SIGRTMAX
```

The actual list of signals varies between Solaris, HP-UX, and Linux.

Default Actions

Every signal has a default action associated with it. The default action for a signal is the action that a script or program performs when it receives a signal.

Some of the possible default actions are –

- Terminate the process.

- Ignore the signal.

- Dump core. This creates a file called core containing the memory image of the process when it received the signal.

- Stop the process.

- Continue a stopped process.

Sending Signals

There are several methods for delivering signals to a program or script. One of the most common is for a user to type CONTROL-C or the INTERRUPT key while a script is executing.

When you press the *Ctrl+C* key a SIGINT is sent to the script and as per the defined default action script terminates.

The other common method for delivering signals is to use the kill command whose syntax is as follows –

```
$ kill -signal pid
```

Here **signal** is either the number or name of the signal to deliver and **pid** is the process ID that the signal should be sent to. For Example –

```
$ kill -1 1001
```

Sends the HUP or hang-up signal to the program that is running with process ID 1001. To send a kill signal to the same process use the following command –

```
$ kill -9 1001
```

This would kill the process running with process ID 1001.

Trapping Signals

When you press the *Ctrl+C* or Break key at your terminal during execution of a shell program, normally that program is immediately terminated, and your command prompt returned. This may not always be desirable. For instance, you may end up leaving a bunch of temporary files that will not get cleaned up.

Trapping these signals is quite easy, the `trap` command has the following syntax –

```
$ trap commands signals
```

Here *command* can be any valid Unix command, or even a user-defined function, and signal can be a list of any number of signals you want to trap.

There are three common uses for trap in shell scripts –

- Clean up temporary files

- Ignore signals

Cleaning Up Temporary Files

As an example of the trap command, the following shows how you can remove files and then exit if someone tries to abort the program from the terminal –

```
$ trap "rm -f $WORKDIR/work1$$ $WORKDIR/dataout$$;
exit" 2
```

From the point in the shell program that this trap is executed, the two files *work1$$* and*dataout$$* will be automatically removed if signal number 2 is received by the program. Therefore, if the user interrupts execution of the program after this trap is executed, you can be assured that these two files will be cleaned up. The **exit** command that follows the rm is necessary because without it execution would continue in the program at the point that it left off when the signal was received.

Signal number 1 is generated for hangup: Either someone intentionally hangs up the line or the line gets accidentally disconnected. You can modify the preceding trap to also remove the two specified files in this case by adding signal number 1 to the list of signals –$ trap "rm $WORKDIR/work1$$ $WORKDIR/dataout$$; exit" 1 2. Now these files will be removed if the line gets hung up or if the *Ctrl+C* key gets pressed. The commands specified to trap must be enclosed in quotes if they contain more than one command. Also, note that the shell scans the command line at the time that the trap command gets executed and also when one of the listed signals is received.

So in the preceding example, the value of WORKDIR and $$ will be substituted at the time that the trap command is executed. If you wanted this substitution to occur at the time that either signal 1 or 2 was received you can put the commands inside single quotes –

```
$ trap 'rm $WORKDIR/work1$$ $WORKDIR/dataout$$; exit' 1 2
```

Ignoring Signals

If the command listed for trap is null, the specified signal will be ignored when received. For example, the command –

```
$ trap '' 2
```

Specifies that the interrupt signal be ignored. You might want to ignore certain signals when performing some operations that you do not want interrupted. You can specify multiple signals to be ignored as follows –

```
$ trap '' 1 2 3 15
```

Note that the first argument must be specified for a signal to be ignored and is not equivalent to writing the following, which has a separate meaning of its own –

```
$ trap   2
```

If you ignore a signal, all subshells also ignore that signal. However, if you specify an action to be taken on receipt of a signal, all subshells will still take the default action on receipt of that signal.

Resetting Traps

After you have changed the default action to be taken on receipt of a signal, you can change it back again with trap if you simply omit the first argument; so.

```
$ trap 1 2
```

Resets the action to be taken on receipt of signals 1 or 2 back to the default.

www.ingramcontent.com/pod-product-compliance
Lightning Source LLC
Chambersburg PA
CBHW071412050326
40689CB00010B/1837